House Broken

House Broken

How I Remodeled My Home for Just
Under Three Times the Original Bid

Richard Karn

with George Mair

HarperEntertainment
A Division of HarperCollinsPublishers

HOUSE BROKEN. Copyright © 1999 by Richard Karn and George Mair. All rights reserved. Printed in the United States of America. No part of this book may be used or reproduced in any manner whatsoever without written permission except in the case of brief quotations embodied in critical articles and reviews. For information address HarperCollins Publishers Inc., 10 East 53rd Street, New York, NY 10022–5299.

HarperEntertainment books may be purchased for educational, business, or sales promotional use. For information please write: Special Markets Department, HarperCollins Publishers Inc., 10 East 53rd Street, New York, NY 10022–5299.

FIRST EDITION

Designed by Charles Kreloff

Library of Congress Cataloging-in-Publication Data is available.
ISBN 0-06-105144-6
99 00 01 02 03 10 9 8 7 6 5 4 3 2 1

To my mother, Louise Wilson,
for always believing in me.

To my father, Gene Wilson,
for giving me common sense and the
ability to laugh at myself when I color outside
the lines.

To my wife, Tudi,
for taking this walk with me through life
and pointing out which roses to smell.

To my son, Cooper,
for asking all the tough questions simply.

Contents

Acknowledgments

A lot of time, good intentions, and money went into the building of my house. The same is true for this book. On the former, I had Tom Callaway and Marty Perry. Tom, our designer, brought with him style, grace, and beautiful ideas, and made it look like they were always there. Marty, our contractor, who had the tough job of telling me what my ideas would cost, brought with him skill, craftsmanship, and the ability to make Tom's ideas work.

On the latter project, I had the great people at HarperCollins Publishers, who decided to take a chance on me. Mauro DiPreta, my editor, gave the book its great look and kept the thrust of it always moving forward. Anja Schmidt answered all my questions and showed me the ropes and how to jump through them.

In between these two projects are the people who made the bridges so all this could happen. Marcia Hurwitz, my wonderful agent, who has made *so* many things happen, introduced me to Susan Crawford, who instantly believed in my idea for the book. She immediately set up meetings with publishers and introduced me to writer George Mair. George, God bless him, spent months burning the midnight oil, putting pen to paper, and giving my rambling some sort of form. He helped me find my voice in print and added his years of experience in the process.

To all of you, I say *thank you*.

INTRODUCTION
Me and My Alter Ego, Al Borland

If you wanted someone to remodel your house, who would you choose—Tim Taylor or Al Borland? Well, if you're like most people, you'd choose Al Borland, because he knows what he's doing. And, after eight years of playing Al, the plaid-shirted, competent one on *Home Improvement*, I would have to agree. He's the right man with the right tools for the job. He cares, he's sensitive, he's inexpensive, and, luckily, I know just how to get in touch with him.

Al Borland evolved over the years as the writers observed the audience and watched Tim and Al interact. *Home Improvement* premiered on ABC in the fall of 1991 and the show was an instant hit. But even as this phenomenon was unfolding in the first season or two, I wasn't always aware of it, and it took a little time to realize how powerful the TV medium really is. I went from, "Aren't you that guy?" to "Aren't you Al?" to "Aren't you Richard?"

Of course, *Tool Time* is the name of the TV show in which Tim and I appear on *Home Improvement*. It is, as I said, a TV show about a TV show. Early in the show's run, I wasn't aware of the public identification of me as Al Borland. It wasn't something that was in the front of my mind yet. After all, I had acted on and off Broadway for about eleven years before I got this TV role, so I still felt anonymous. But that was changing. I guess one of the first clues came the day I was in an airport in

Florida. My plane was canceled, so I had to change to another.

The lady at the counter was beaming as I was walking up because she recognized me. She said, "Could you sign this? My husband loves your show."

Almost immediately after that, I was engulfed by thirty or forty cheerleaders who overheard this innocent exchange while they were waiting for their flight. It was like a surreal TV commercial happening and involving me. It was the weirdest feeling. I felt like birdseed.

Over the years, I have been asked by different interviewers what makes Al Borland so popular. Number one: good writing. Number two: no matter how silly the situation, he always keeps his dignity. Number three: those plaid shirts. He's an average guy: not a star, just an ordinary, nice guy trying to do his job as best he can—innocent and a little guileless.

I've tried to make him as real as possible so he comes to things with a lot of naïveté. Beyond that, I think people appreciate that Al Borland does his job well, even though his boss doesn't always appreciate him.

After the first year of the show, my character evolved as the writers watched the audience watch Tim Allen and me bring their words to life. And as we got away from the workplace where he's very competent and secure in his knowledge of craftmanship, we started to find out he's a little awkward in social situations. For situation comedy to work, sometimes you have to be just plain dumb so that a lesson can be learned. The fine line is being able to play dumb while, at the same time, keeping your sense of self. In a lot of ways, Al's like my dad, who happens to be a builder and a contractor—quiet but very competent. He's

> If you can smile when things go wrong, you have someone in mind to blame.

not a showboater, he's just very good. Tim's more of the show-man. When Tim tries to show off—maybe he's going to break something or whatever—Al steps in to pick up the pieces.

The original concept of Tim's assistant was different. He was older, taller, balding, and more irascible. The kind of guy whose ulcer flared every time Tim screwed up. Also different was Al's now-famous retort to Tim's mistakes: "I don't think so." I took it and made it more important than it was. With that line, I unknowingly took a one-dimensional thing off the page and made it into a three-year relationship between the charac-ter and me. It hasn't become the most famous line in acting—a recent survey picked "Bond, James Bond" for that accolade—but it certainly is popular. In fact, the Al Borland character is so popular that the people who rate these things (they call them Q ratings and they indicate the level of public acceptance of various characters and actors), say that I am the second most likable man on prime-time TV. That's very flattering. When I saw those numbers, my jaw dropped. To be more rec-ognized than Andy Griffith and Jerry Seinfeld is a little scary. In fact, the image of me in a plaid shirt is so valuable that the pro-ducers of the show, Disney, copyrighted it. Which means, I suppose, that every time I go to the supermarket in a plaid shirt, Disney could demand a royalty.

This popularity did not go unnoticed as I was getting calls from different companies to represent them, and I also got a call from Underwiters Laboratories Inc. saying they would like me to be their safety spokesman. They brought me to Washington, D.C., and I got a tour of the White House. The first stop on my tour of the White House was the carpenter's shop downstairs, where they showed me all the different shovels used to plant different trees on the grounds. At the time, they were also building a bookcase for Chelsea Clinton and repair-ing a desk from the Lincoln Bedroom.

Practically everyone on *Home Improvement*, the show, has been involved in home improvement, the reality, and they all had various stories and anecdotes. Tim's always seemed to center on lighting.

His house is built on an acre and he has a big backyard. He put in these beautiful garden lights that kept shorting out. When he asked his contractor about it, the contractor replied, "Well, they're not supposed to get *wet!*"

"What do you mean they're not supposed to get wet? They're outside lighting."

"Oh, you wanted *waterproof* lighting!

"What's the difference?"

"Well, waterproof lighting can get wet."

"So, outdoor lighting can't get wet?"

Historic Building Blunders

The White House and Blair House

The White House was built over what had been originally a swamp, in a locale where the summers were so bad, the inhabitants had to move to other quarters elsewhere in Washington. In fact, one of Lincoln's children died in the White House because of swamp fever. As a result of the swampy foundation base, the White House has been gradually sinking a

"Noooo, you don't want to get them wet!"

"But, you put them in the garden."

"Well, they're not supposed to get *wet*."

"But, they're in the garden."

"Yeah! That's why they're shorting out."

He also put some very expensive halogen lights in his car showroom. Every time he would visit the showroom, there would be eight or nine of these very expensive lights out. Here again, he brought it up with his contractor.

"Boy, these things burn out," Tim remarked.

"Well, they're not supposed to be on," the contractor replied.

"What do you mean, 'They're not supposed to be on'?"

"Well, they're just to turn on, do what you need to do, and turn off."

fraction of an inch each year. The same is true of the Washington Monument. Finally, during Harry Truman's term in office, the First Family moved out to the Blair House across Pennsylvania Avenue. The Blair House has been the official residence for visiting dignitaries over the years, and it, too, was deteriorating, with the flooding of the basement, garage, and elevator shafts. Also, the roof and air-conditioning leaked and was damaging walls and carpeting, while there were also serious problems with the hot water system and heating. By 1982 it got to the point that the Blair House was closed for $7 million in emergency repairs. What happened to finally move the government to remodeling was the chandelier in the master bedroom dropping from the ceiling and onto the bed, which, fortunately, was unoccupied at the time.

"It's a *show* room. The lights need to be on."

"Well, they're not built to be on. It'll wear them out."

And then, by sheer coincidence, he discovered there was one section of the outside lights that was making a line on his TV screen.

"So, the outside lights are affecting my television set," Tim said.

"Well, not all of them. Just one section," the contractor answered.

"So, you're telling me that I have to turn the lights out to watch TV?"

"Yup."

"Why is this happening?"

"I don't know, I have never seen anything like this before in my twenty-five years. . . ."

A Simple
Idea

On Time and Under Budget— I Don't Think So

> "We were standing in the hall of our newly remodeled house just soaking it all in and Rick said, 'Well, you know, when we do our next house . . .' I jumped in immediately and said, 'Honey, look in my eyes! Right here in my eyes! We will live our lives, hopefully to a ripe old age, and we will die in this house. We are never going to move to another house or remodel again!'"
>
> —my wife, Tudi

It was a simple idea that became an amazing, uh, adventure.

I was standing in the middle of a house that I paid a lot of money for and there was no ceiling. I could see the entire house because the walls were gone. There was no flooring. The kitchen couldn't be used, and there was no working toilet. I stood there knee-deep in my ideas and tried to remember how I got here. Suddenly, I began laughing. Anyone on the outside would've thought I'd lost my mind, which wouldn't have been too far from the truth. But, in reality, I had something on the inside click, melding life and art in a struggle that hasn't occurred in my life since the fifth-grade Thanksgiving Day play.

Then, I stood in the wings of the cafeteria stage on a cold October morning, very nervous and thinking that I could just turn around, walk down those stairs, out the door, and never look back. As I considered that option, I stepped through my paralysis and onto the stage and started a series of events that would be my life. To this day, I still have that exact thought before I do anything that really means something to me. At this moment, in the middle of the chaos I called my new home, I decided to walk onto that stage merging art and life in a project of epic proportions. I realized that this really meant something to me.

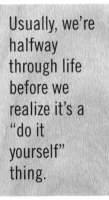

Usually, we're halfway through life before we realize it's a "do it yourself" thing.

However, for me, art would not exactly imitate life. Al Borland of *Home Improvement* is a better man than I. Still, I am the son of a builder, not to mention the grandson of a builder and the great-grandson of a builder. Building is in my blood so I should know how to do this. Right? And, because of the role I play and because of the heritage I was born into, I would sidestep the problems other people would encounter. I would find the right people for the right job and get it done right away. Boy, was I naïve.

Perhaps it's best at this point if we go back to the beginning.

The Great American House Hunt and Nesting Ritual

The First Home

grew up in a house, always lived in a house, always pictured myself living in a house. I never pictured myself living in an apartment, even though I lived in apartments in New York and Los Angeles for thirteen years. After finishing the first season on *Home Improvement*, we felt we could buy a house and were in a unique situation where we didn't have to buy a starter house. Unlike many young couples, we could skip that "starter home." You know, the one with the coal-powered kitchen appliances, a bathroom that's really an outhouse, and a smell in the basement that makes you uneasy because you can never figure out its source.

One frustration is that movies and television have just ruined everyone's perspective on living space. On TV you have these struggling young people living in a loft in Manhattan that in reality is something like $5,000 a month and they're only paying twenty dollars. "Oh, it's just this little loft I found and fixed it up." Sure. So the reality about what you can actually afford is sometimes a little scary. But we'd look at houses and say, "Oh, yeah, we can make this work."

Even though we had a Realtor, sometimes we went out on our own and looked on weekends because you never know what you're going to find, and that's when we found the Magnolia

> Duct tape is like the Force in *Star Wars.* It has a light side, a dark side, and it holds the universe together.

Avenue house. (I don't know about you, but we named all the houses we looked at and liked after the streets they were on.)

The house, when we first saw it, was in a cozy little neighborhood, with a garage on one side and a couple of windows on the other, a door in the middle, and dormers on top so it looked like there might be a bedroom upstairs. It didn't seem like such a big house, but, in Hollywood, nothing is ever as it seems.

So, from the outside it looked like a little Cape Cod, but as soon as we walked in that front door, we immediately realized this was out of our league. It was really nice. Everything was done, and it was in move-in condition. There were two more bedrooms than we thought there were going to be. This was not an "off the rack" house. It was custom fit to us.

It was also the kind of house that we probably wouldn't have even gone inside to see if we'd known the price beforehand. And, of course, we ended up buying it.

It had everything we wanted. We went right down our list. It even had things that we didn't know we wanted, such as being completely childproofed. With our son, Cooper, newly arrived, this was important. All the doors, cabinets, and drawers had those little latches that made them childproof. (It was a little embarrassing, of course, that we couldn't work the childproof toilet seat at first.) Plus the nursery was already decorated—it had everything. And, to top it off, the house had good Hollywood karma because the owners had written *Cheers* for the last five years in their office upstairs.

When we moved in, Tudi and I believed we were going to live in that house for the rest of our lives. If we had only known then what we know now. After we bought it, I walked around saying, "I own that, I own this, I can change this, I can do that because this is my house—I own it." Four years later I look back and realize you never really "own" anything. You just borrow it for a while.

The Search for Gated Happiness

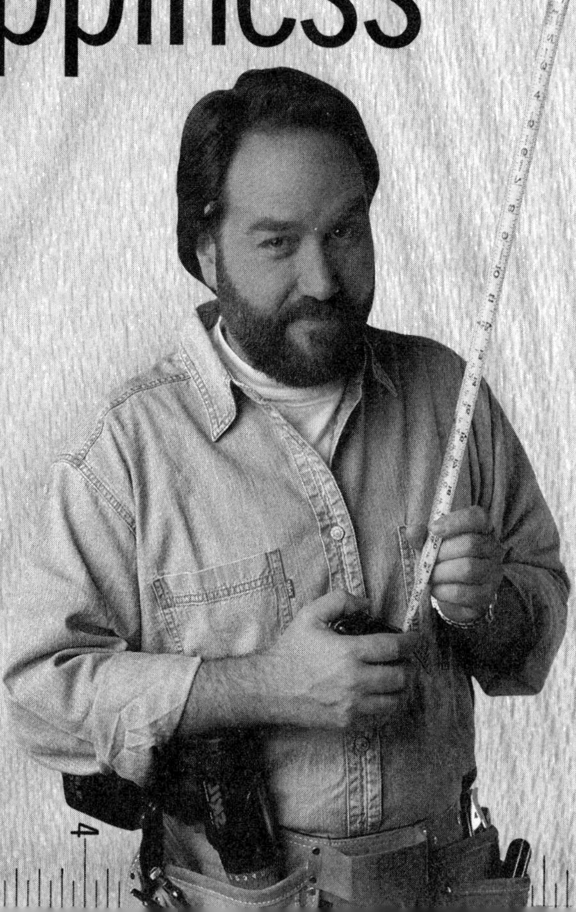

After a few years it became apparent—first to Tudi and then to myself (things tend to become apparent to Tudi before they become apparent to me)—that we needed more security. Also, a bigger backyard would have been nice. So we set out to look for another house.

This time we were very specific about what we wanted, as contrasted with the last house hunt, when we were more general in our list of "must-haves" and "would-be-nice-if-it-hads." We knew we could spend a little more money. We knew we wanted a bigger backyard. We knew we wanted a fence and a gate. We knew we wanted a couple of extra bedrooms for visiting family. And we knew we wanted it at the same price we paid for our first house. Made sense to us. We wanted twice the house and the same price.

But now we encountered a strange phenomenon: there was a big jump in the prices of the houses the Realtor was showing us and, I swear, the houses looked worse. Sure, the lots were a little bigger, but the houses were really tacky, with excess money spent on things you didn't really need. You know, five different wet bars with solid gold faucets. All these extra gadgets and fancy materials made the houses more expensive, but not nicer living spaces.

California is so multicultural, and so many creative people from the movies and television who had money to spend have lived there over the years, that you can actually find just about anything you want if you're willing to look for it. The trick is to find everything you want under one sky. The story of Pickfair is an example. Douglas Fairbanks and Mary Pickford built their house while they had their own movie studio. They would use their studio workers to build their house and, at one point, it was being built twenty-four hours a day—around the clock. They brought in fifty-foot trees and built everything like it had been there forever—just like a movie set. That was something we couldn't afford.

We began by sorting out our priorities. For Tudi, a secure home that was fenced and gated was essential. For me, I really wanted a place near the water, because I grew up in Washington State, where the water is either on you or vice versa. Tudi grew up in West Texas, so she didn't know about water until she was sixteen. She says the town she was raised in was so flat, you could stand on a tuna can and see across it. The main body of water in town was Lake Nasworthy, which she and the other kids nicknamed Nasty Water.

However, much as I wanted to be near the water, it wasn't practical. My work is at the Disney Studios in Burbank, about twenty miles from the water or two days by car in traffic, so we first started looking for a home in the surrounding area. After several weeks we couldn't find what we wanted, so we expanded our horizons into another community, a lovely suburb located about two miles beyond our income.

The important thing was to find a real estate agent who knew the area.

> Some tribes in the Sahara Desert build their homes out of camel dung and chicken wire. They're light enough to be strapped on a camel's back and moved to a new location whenever needed.

We connected with Nina, and from her we learned a lot of things about houses and real estate. First, we learned that most real estate agents are a combination tour guide, friendly chat-up, high-pressure salesman, and charming confidant.

We began our search for gated happiness with the normal get-acquainted routine by telling Nina the kind of home we wanted and what we wanted to pay. This was followed by hysterical laughter from Nina, who told me she enjoyed watching me on *Home Improvement* and never realized I was so funny in person.

Soon, Nina began taking us house hunting to see the available listings. The idea was to "orient" us. This is a Realtor code word for convincing us the closest we were going to find to what we had in mind in our price range was in remote portions of Asia. The more time we spent driving around looking at houses in L.A., the more real estate jargon we picked up. Here are some of the highlights:

- Maintenance-free: means a place that hasn't had a paint job or anything else in twenty-five years. It has been free of maintenance.

- Robin Hood House: This is not a romantic cottage in a forest. It's a place with a Little John.

- Charming: Too small. Synonyms include, "cute, "enchanting," and "good starter home."

- Rustic: old and out-of-date.

- Family house: it has more than one bathroom—barely.

- Unique Urban Home: used to be a warehouse.

- Daring Design: still is a warehouse.

- Sophisticated: has avocado dishwashers, shag carpeting, black walls, no windows, and lava lamps throughout.

- New Listing: a house you see accidentally and the agent didn't show you. She always explains, "Oh, it just came on the market. I forgot to tell you about it."

- Fixer-Upper: a grimly infamous place you don't want to go.

- Much Potential: synonym for "Fixer-Upper."

- One-of-a-Kind: ugly beyond belief and in violation of the health code.

- Brilliant Concept: house with a live tree growing through the ceiling of the living room.

- Must See It to Believe It: the one really accurate real estate description. This place usually provides you with amusing dinner conversation for the next three months.

One method we could have tried to realize our dream house is the Hypnosis Walk Through that, it's claimed, brings out the factors that trigger buying decisions. Apparently, there are hypnotists who do this Hypnosis Walk Through for people. In its simplicity, the hypnotist puts you under hypnosis and then has you describe a room-by-room walk through your dream house. I am sure you would want to have your significant other in the room and not under hypnosis while you underwent this, if you were brave enough to try. That would be to keep you from buying a house the hypnotist wanted to sell you.

After we'd been out on several of these expeditions, our expectations began to get more realistic, which is exactly why the agent trotted us around to see a lot of unsuitable but, sometimes, fascinating properties. I believe that houses for sale are extensions of the personalities of the people who have left them. For example, one property we visited was almost garish in architectural style, down to an entrance flanked by flaming torches. It looked like an overblown Mexican restaurant, and as we drove up, I half expected a parking valet to appear in a black bolero jacket. Maybe he was trying out his restaurant renovations on his own home.

As Tudi says, when we first looked for a house, we weren't in a hurry. We looked for almost nine months, which reminded us of another kind of gestation period that would be oddly analogous because, in some ways, our new house would be a new baby. It would be the fulfillment of some dreams; it would involve a lot of changes; it might help or endanger our marriage; and it would cost a lot more than we ever anticipated both to raze it and to raise it.

One important lesson we learned in our search was that most real estate is whatever is out there at the moment you're looking, and how you perceive it. So if you buy a house and a really great house comes up (later), you've missed that. Another way to miss a house is to think it's either over or under your price range. I heard about this house on Toluca Lake that was for sale when we were looking. However, it was listed at three million dollars, which was higher than we felt comfortable with, so we passed on looking at it. I found out later it sold for $1.1 million. At that selling price, we might have been interested. I kicked myself for not following up on it.

Ultimately, the selection of a new home is as much a function of stamina as choice and judgment. All the time in the world can be too much, and if you have to be out of your existing house by the end of the month, it can be too little. For us, the search took nine months, and, as I said, it was time to deliver the baby. We kept looking and looking, and finally we found a place that, on paper, sounded perfect. Coincidentally, as we're walking into it, one of the writers on *Home Improvement*, Roz Moore, was walking out.

I had a moment of anxiety that we'd missed out. I asked her, nervously, thinking she'd want it for herself, "What did you think?"

"Well, it's kind of a weird layout. Not for me," she said off-handedly.

"Really? It's not for you? Okay. That's too bad."

I was relieved.

We sympathized but secretly still wanted to take a look for ourselves. However, Roz was right, it was kind of a weird layout. There wasn't a normal flow from room to room, and each room had a different style. Some rooms had dark wood, some rooms had light wood, some rooms had painted wood, and some rooms had whitewashed wood. Nothing was really connected, but it had lots of room. The backyard was huge, and the front yard had a gate. It had all thing things we wanted—all the bones were right. We said to ourselves, "All we really need to do is retile the kitchen and, maybe, add on to the master bedroom—make it a little bigger and give it a cathedral ceiling." We had a cathedral ceiling where we were, and we really liked that. And that's all that we set out to do—retile the kitchen and add on to the master bedroom.

Thinking back on the year and a half of remodeling after the nine months of house hunting, the house had all the things we wanted without a style. The house was just kind of blah and I wonder now what it was that attracted us. I'm not sure, because we changed everything. What was it that really drew us? Maybe I'll never know.

Making a Deal and Getting Escrowed

Now that we had found the house we wanted, it came time to sit down and work out a deal. When we got to the Realtor's office to negotiate, the office looked really, really nice, which is supposed to allow you to feel comfortable and secure, but it only made me think that these guys were making a lot of money. We ironed out the details and the deal was finally signed and sealed. Then, to officially buy the house, we went through a mystical process called "escrow," which, considering what happens, may be either a noun or a verb. In any case, we signed a huge number of documents, most of which we didn't read and many of which we didn't understand. It wasn't as regal a ceremony as the Japanese surrender on the deck of the USS *Missouri* ending World War II. Unlike the Japanese, though, we had to sign everything in triplicate.

In this process, you give people enormous amounts of money but nobody seems to believe you are who you are. So you show your driver's license to a total stranger, and she suddenly vouches for you being you, and everybody believes this person you have never seen before and, likely, will never see again. She even affixes an official-looking seal on some of the documents under the title of notary public. Suddenly, we were "home owners"—squared. We owned two homes. Actually, the bank owned two homes, and our mission, were we to choose to accept it, was to make the payments on both of them.

Since we were living in our old Magnolia Avenue house while the new house would be undergoing "minor remodeling," I suggested to Tudi that we sell the old Magnolia Avenue house and live in our new house. After all, we were only going to redo the master bedroom and the tile in the kitchen, and selling the old house would save money. In her shy way, she understood what could happen if we did that and firmly said "No!" Once again she had the sense to know it was a bad idea.

What we came down to is, we were going to expand the master bedroom, which also meant we had to take away the old bathroom in the room designated for our son, Cooper, and we were going to redo the kitchen . . . actually, just the tile. We discussed doing the cabinets and everything, but thought, "Aw, someday, someday."

Rick's House Hunting Secrets

Experts say that, whether or not we realize it, most of us subconsciously decide on buying a house within the first fifteen minutes we see it. It isn't the physical that captures our mind and emotions as much as the intuitive and psychological. When Tudi, my son, and I looked at the house we bought, Tudi had, I think unbeknownst to any of us, decided on that house. So we went back to our old Magnolia Avenue house and Tudi told me and my son to stay there. She went back to the house to look again. She was going back to look around once more and start the remodeling in her head.

Now, while impulse buying may sound romantic, it can have serious and costly drawbacks. Here are my personal tips on what you should check before signing that check:

CURB APPEAL: Take time to study the house from the street to get an over-all impression of the image it presents both on the property and in the neighborhood. Some day you may be selling instead of buying, and this curb appeal is an important first-impression factor.

DRAINAGE: In ancient days, tribes would camp on high ground so water wouldn't drain into their tepees and cause problems. Follow the same concept in your tepee. The grounds, driveways, and outdoor areas should drain away from the house at least a foot for every six-foot distance from the foundation. In the house that we bought and remodeled, the previous owner added a den, which we converted into a media room and, for some reason I can't figure out, made it two steps down from the ground level of the rest of the house. So we had to be careful that there was no water drainage that might flood this room, though I'm sure Cooper might enjoy having a trout pond in this back room. In any case, check for possible drainage problems, otherwise, there will be flooded basements, foundation erosion, and a lot of other annoyances—expensive annoyances.

TREES AND FOLIAGE: Big trees can enhance the house's appearance and give shade when it's hot, but their roots can also disrupt the plumbing lines and the foundation if the trees are too close to the house—too close is probably less than ten feet. The same with some foliage and bushes. Security experts say to avoid anything that allows a burglar to be screened from observers on the street as he breaks into your home.

One secret way of checking the date the house was built is to lift up the top of the toilet tank, assuming it is the original plumbing and not a replacement. On the underside of the toilet tank lid is a date stamped telling when that unit was manufactured and it's usually within a few months of when it was installed in the house.

Historic Building Blunders

Collapsing Roof

In spite of building in areas known for heavy rain or snow, some developers and contractors don't provide for the weight stress or drainage necessary that make for spectacular roof collapses. In Kansas City, the roof of the 17,600-seat Kemper Arena crashed ninety-five feet to the empty main floor. As the acre-size roof plunged downward, it acted like a gigantic piston and raised the interior air pressure so high that it blew out the walls of the building. The cause was the failure of several bolts holding up the roof.

On Long Island University's C.W. Post College campus, the Dome Auditorium's roof cracked like a giant eggshell and collapsed under a load of snow and ice in the middle of the night on January 21, 1978. The cause was a design failure that created a dome that would hold up a load of snow four times what it was on January twenty-first, *provided the snow was evenly distributed,* which it wasn't.

The Allied Roofing and Siding Company in Grand Rapids, Michigan, did a big business in 1979 clearing snow from the roofs of clients so they would not be damaged or collapse. It was just about this time that the roof of the Allied Roofing and Siding Company collapsed from the weight of too much snow.

After all, if he's taking the trouble to break in, you might as well let the neighbors enjoy the view.

ROOF: Obviously, you will ultimately have to get up on the roof or have someone go up there for you to check if it is sound and leakproof. But even from the ground level you can note if shingles or other roof covering are not lying flat and snug or if the roof seems to sag. Both are warning signs. If some parts of the roof are a different color from the rest of it, it may mean repairs have been done, and that should alert you to a possible problem. Asphalt shingles are good for about twenty-five years; wood shake singles, forty; and tile somewhere in between. So check when the house was built, and it will give you an idea of how many years the roof probably has left.

WALLS: Look for signs that the outside walls are not snug and tight against the framework of the house. On brick and masonry walls, poke around at the mortar with a knife or nail file to see if the mortar is crumbling. That is a sure sign mortar termites have been there. Next, stand at a corner of the house and sight down the length of walls going in each direction to see if you can detect sagging. That could mean big trouble with the underlying structure.

If you haven't figured out the basic rule of home repair: Big Trouble = Big Money.

What the Broker and Seller Don't Want You to Know

Our experience in looking at scores of properties and purchasing two houses taught us some truths about home buying. First, the broker is working for the seller. The broker has a signed contract with the home owner, who agrees to pay him a percentage of the sale price if the broker produces a buyer. You are just one of many prospects the broker has in tow. The oddity of this is that home seekers become friendly with the broker and begin asking the broker's advice and guidance on how to make a deal with the seller. This is like talking with the opposing lawyer in a court case to find out what the other side will settle for in the lawsuit. So keep your own counsel, and if you feel you need advice, hire another broker for a fee to represent you.

Second, as I said, finding a house is all in the timing. You depend mostly on the houses that are listed with the real estate brokers' multiple listing service. You look through what is available and bid on that even though the "perfect house" may come into the listing pool the next day.

Third, it is always wise to make your deal contingent on having the property inspected by an engineer of *your* choosing to detect any obvious structural defects that might cost you *mucho dinero* (some of the Spanish I have learned since moving to California). Our designer on this project, Tom, echoes that advice because he doesn't believe many inspectors have the time or are paid enough to really probe beyond the surface appearances of the property. So pick an inspector very carefully, and don't just go along with the broker or escrow agent's choice—they have a vested interest in a quick and rosy report from an inspector they know. That kind of inspector is probably more loyal to them than to you because he gets lots of business from them and this is probably the only job he'll ever do for you. Also, you should go on the inspection tour with the inspector and inspect the inspector doing the inspection. (Whew!) That way, you can get answers on the spot about things you may find that trouble you. We agreed to the inspector picked by other people, and it seems as if he missed some things with us such as the illegal aluminum gas line. Of course, in fairness, it is not possible for an inspector to catch everything. Some things might be buried underground or in the building walls, but a good inspector is worth the money and will cost a lot less money than a bad inspection could cost you in repairs.

Next, be careful when a broker tries to push you into making an offer on a property that he or she labels as "a steal." If it is a steal, make sure you know who is going to be the stealer and who is going to be the stealee.

> We bought this dream house and it was like getting involved in a relationship— you find the perfect mate and instantly try to change him or her.

Also, there is sometimes a quicksand trap you should know about called the infamous "Disclosure List." At the closing of the deal, a "Disclosure List" is often required of the seller. In it, the seller specifies anything significant on the property that is not working properly. When we bought our first house, the sellers listed an appliance called Mr. Steam. They said it didn't work and they would not fix it since it was broken when they moved in and they'd never used it. We never used it or fixed it either, but when it came to our selling, we forgot to disclose it was broken. Suddenly, we were expected to fix Mr. Steam. That was just because of our ignorance, but it was another lesson learned. The appliance may never have been used, but it did get us a little steamed after all.

Finally, there is a money tip that we probably should print on an asbestos page because real estate brokers will want to burn this. The six-percent commission on the sale of the property is not sacred and can often be negotiated down.

We Begin Our Adventure

Mr. Blandings Builds His Dream House Meets The Twilight Zone

H aving three generations of builders behind me, and fast becoming the go-to man in the how-to world, I figured our remodeling would be a piece of cake, but I didn't think we'd have to buy the bakery in the process. I know my dad never thought I would get involved in construction work, and his mom, my grandmother, was adamantly opposed to the idea. Grandma was helping me memorize my lines for the infamous Thanksgiving Day play when she told me for the first time that if I ever became a builder, she'd wrap me in cement and throw me in the lake. Her husband and her son were both builders and I guess she wanted me to do something else. I can't help but think what Grandma would have done with me today, after I got involved in our gigantic remodeling project: probably wrap me in a blanket and throw me in the nearby Los Angeles River, where I would probably choke to death on the dust, since it rarely has any water in it.

Still, there is some consolation in the fact that millions of Americans spend $100 billion—that's with a B as in Boy-o-Boy—every year going through the same thing we did. While many of them don't remember the 1946 Cary Grant comedy, *Mr. Blandings Builds His Dream House*, or Rod Serling's sci-fi TV show, *The Twilight Zone*, those were the two worlds we entered—both comic and eerie. If it wasn't for a sense of humor about our own suburban adventure, Tudi and I might not have survived. Certainly, the kitchen would have been painted a different color.

My confidence in doing a remodeling job stemmed from the long history of the men in my family, who have been builders going back to the early days of my hometown, Seattle. Coincidental to Seattle being my hometown, it's also the hometown of the richest man in the world, Bill Gates. He and I have several things in common: we're both from Seattle and we both got involved in a major home improvement project. Of course, there are some minor differences in that he's a billionaire and his home has thirty garages and is about a thousand times bigger than mine.

In Chicago it had been Mrs. O'Leary's cow and a lantern. In Seattle it was the glue pot in a carpenter's shop. Both were trivial accidents that shaped a city.

It was two-thirty on the afternoon of June 6, 1889, when the glue pot in the carpenter's basement shop on Front Street caught fire. In minutes the flames tongued out to engulf the scores of wooden buildings that had grown from the few cabins built around Henry Yelser's sawmill. In 1851, those wooden buildings had spawned this bawdy northwestern town named after Indian chief Sealth. Before the sun set on that cataclysmic day, the sixty-four-acre Seattle business district had been transformed into a smoldering plain of ash, filling the air with acrid smoke and lungs with pungent odors.

The frontier spirit of the 42,000 residents of Seattle stiffened with a determination to rebuild their city and seize the opportunity to design it better. They set about moving buildings and dirt to create a sensible city plan. Where the land wasn't level, men with teams of horses and earth-moving equipment made it level, as in the case of 107-foot-high Denny Hill. The immense volume of dirt from Denny Hill, for example, was needed at the water's edge to create a suitable harbor and mooring for oceangoing ships. This was the kind of hard scrabble work that required men like my great-grandfather Wilson.

That's how it started for Seattle, and that was the Seattle in which I started as Richard Karn Wilson in 1956. As you see, my forefathers were there when Seattle was being put together over a hundred years ago and helped build the town. But to get there our forefathers and foremothers had to make the great trek across the central plains from Minnesota and eastern Canada. As the family story goes, one of my great-great-great grandmothers, coming across the country in a covered wagon, gave food and coffee grounds to the Indians as they went along. It must have paid off because, at some point, one of the squaws came by and told her to hide quickly. Warned of danger, she hid just before an Indian attack in what became known as the Yellow Medicine Massacre. So, giving away coffee grounds may have been one of the early acts of serendipity that would set the course of life for the Wilsons and, ultimately, for me.

So it was that my forefathers and foremothers came to Seattle, where most of them would go into the construction business—until I came along and became an actor. After growing up and graduating from the University of Washington, I went to New York to pursue my career and the beautiful actress from Texas, Tudi, who became my wife. In time we realized that Hollywood was the best place for our professional careers, and we moved west in search of roles.

It was during this time my good luck muse, Serendipity, would reappear, the planets would realign, Mercury would ascend, and my life would change dramatically once again. Most people don't know it, but there is a lot of baggage that comes with doing *Macbeth*. In fact, it is an old theater superstition that one must never mention the name *Macbeth*, and only refer to it as "the Scottish Play." The reason is that every production of *Macbeth* has had bad luck attached to it because of the witches' incantations in the play.

It all started when I did what we Californians call a

"California stop." The term, a well-established phenomenon, consists, in rapid succession, of: (1) glancing briefly at the red octagonal sign by the road; (2) concluding immediately that this is a stupid place for a stop sign; (3) touching the brake pedal oh so gently, to demonstrate to the car and the world that you could stop if you *really* had to; and finally, (4) realizing that you are now in the middle of the intersection and to stop would create a traffic hazard. As a good citizen, you continue on through the intersection so as not to be a public danger. A lesser known step is #5, which consists of coming to a full stop and producing your driver's license and car registration for the officer in blue.

This explains why I ended up in traffic school to avoid a bad mark on my driving record. As I entered the traffic school classroom, I spotted an open seat next to a nice-looking woman who I didn't realize at the moment was my old friend, Serendipity. I sat, we talked, and it developed that she was an agent. As we talked further, she told me some producers I knew were casting a show for ABC-TV called *Home Improvement*. I had worked with these producers, Matt Williams, David McFadzean, and Carmen Finestra, at the New Harmony Theater Festival in Indiana sometime before, so I felt comfortable calling them and asking if there was anything for me. They said there wasn't, but I should come in and audition anyway because there would be guest roles and they wanted me to meet their casting director. I auditioned and made them laugh, which is not an easy thing to do after they'd seen the same scene five hundred times. In other serendipitous coincidences, the woman playing Lady Macbeth with me at the Baptist church was married to the comedy development liaison for the show and for ABC-TV. Also, ten years before, I had worked with John Pasquin, who was now the director of the first episodes of *Home Improvement*. There were so many lucky omens going for me, it would have been criminal if I didn't get something out of the audition. Actually, there were some negatives too—one BIG negative: the role was already cast. At the time, the character's name was not Al Borland, it was Glenn, and the role had been cast with Stephen Topolowsky.

On the flip side, Stephen was also cast in a film role and couldn't get away for the pilot of *Home Improvement.* Because the producers knew me, they could bring me in for the pilot and knew I wouldn't make a big deal out of it if Stephen came back to do the series if it got picked up. Six weeks after my audition, one of the producers, Carmen Finestra, telephoned and said, "I hope you haven't shaved that beard off."

So I came in to do the pilot as a stand-in for Stephen, and they changed the role of Glenn to Al Borland because Glenn was coming back. I figured I was just a temp on the show. However, Stephen kept getting film work—yes!—and putting the producers of *Home Improvement* off. This allowed me to show just how perfect I was for this role. Finally, Tim Allen and the producers decided we were a great working team.

As it was, I did the first five shows just as a guest star before I was made a regular cast member. The characters of Tim and Al clicked right away. Tim and I, on the other hand, took a year or so to get to know one another, but eventually we clicked too.

For five months I didn't know if I would have a regular job. We did the pilot program of *Home Improvement* in April, and soon after we got pregnant. Well, Tudi got pregnant, but I helped. Not knowing if I would eventually become a regular, we spent five months nervous about the fact that we were starting a family without any visible means of support.

Thinking back, I realize that before *Home Improvement,* I was very happy pursuing my career—no desperation. I was in plays and I felt good about the work. I was at a point in my career where anything seemed possible. I wasn't thinking about failure. But then I got this job and I thought, "God, I can't believe how terrifying this profession is. The pure randomness of it is mind-boggling. How does anybody get a job in this world?"

As a kid, it never occurred to me that my parents had these same emotions. On the one side, my mother and grandmother were artists. On the other side, my father, grandfather, and great-grandfather were building contractors who not only built our family home, but all the houses on our block and some on the next street down. They built houses for $9,000 and sold them for $15,000. They were quite prolific.

My grandfather Karn was a piano tuner, and Grandfather Wilson, one of the early Seattle developers, was in the home-moving business. He had a livery stable and used his teams of horses to move earth and buildings around in those early days when Seattle was being designed. As a matter of fact, we still have some of that earth-moving equipment. I think we have all of the tools my family ever had. Which means, after this book, I'm starting a museum. You should know right now that the Wilsons never throw anything out—just ask my wife, Tudi.

However, *Home Improvement* has also had an effect on my building contractor father, Gene Wilson. Since he grew up in Seattle as a builder, all of the lumberyards and hardware stores that knew him now know that he's Al's dad and have a new respect for him . . . which really makes him laugh because he still sees me as the little boy who bends nails every time he picks up a hammer.

Dad has even been in some of our *Home Improvement* shows as a nonspeaking extra. But the best thing is that the show has made him stop worrying about my future. He wouldn't let me know it, but there was a really heavy worry: "What if, as an actor, you don't make it?" I think every father feels that. When I told him about this job, he was like, "Great. That's nice." It wasn't until he actually saw it on television that reality kicked in. Then, as the show got more and more popular, I saw this great relief come over him.

As I said, when my dad visits I am reminded of the different worlds we each now inhabit. He is retired, after spending his life building homes, and he's sort of shy and conservative. I am in the most active phase of my life, an extrovert and outgoing actor. I recall two examples when our respective worlds directly clashed. Once I had my dad do a commercial with me up in Canada. He's out in front of the camera, and the director is trying to get him to be a little more animated and, perhaps, make it look as if he's having a good time talking about the product we were promoting. Finally, the director says to dad, "Mr. Wilson—his name is Wilson—could you smile?"

"I am smiling."

He thought he was smiling, but no one could tell because there was no expression on his face, and he turned to me and asked, "I am smiling, aren't I?"

Then, he sometimes comes over to the studio and he'll sit there and watch rehearsal all week long. He'll sit there. I can't do that. There was one time Bob Vila was on the show and we were putting in a doorjamb. We needed to prop the doorjamb up, but couldn't remember what the prop was called. So one of the writers called over to my dad, who was sitting in the audience, "Gene, what's that called?"

"Well, back where I come from," he said, "that's called a 'cripple.'"

Obviously, in politically sensitive television we couldn't use that word. Just then, Bob Vila remembered that, back where he comes from, its called a "jack stud."

The writers said, "Well, we really can't say 'cripple.'" So, we used Bob Vila's name for it. But it left my father a touch confused because to him "cripple" didn't mean anything bad, it was just what they called a prop like the one we were using.

Of course, Dad's view is different from mine. As he would say, "My going down to see Rick is always a great thing, and I love to go to the studio. I'll sit there and watch them perform all day long. It's something different for me. I've never seen anything like this. I am amazed at their ability to do these things. I have been on several of the shows. There was one where I was a judge and I had the robes on and I was standing up there and I said to myself, 'Now, this is no big deal. How come these guys get paid so much?' Then, it dawned on me that I wasn't saying anything. I was just standing there. Then I thought, 'Well, if I had to say something, I'd be pouring down sweat.'"

Getting It Wrong, But Right

The first major steps in remodeling our new house were to pick a designer and a building contractor. Each has an important role to play: namely, keeping you from doing stupid things and making sure everything is done the way you want it done, even if you don't know the way you want it done. Even with my extensive background in building, I went about this simple initial process wrong.

The house was what we call California ranch style, and we only wanted to do a few things to it to fit our needs. Normally, the sequence would been for us to hire a designer, who usually has a contractor he works with regularly. Instead we began by doing it backward. I found a great contractor first. I asked our assistant director on *Home Improvement* to hook me up with the contractor who had done some work for her parents. I went and looked at Marty's work and said to myself, "Oh, that's pretty nice." When we met him, he seemed very concise and very capable, so we hired him.

About a year earlier we heard about a wonderful designer, Tom, from friends down the street from our old Magnolia Avenue house, Shelly and Mike Farrell. Tom had done a terrific job with their house, so when it came time for our remodeling, we knew we wanted his experience and great ideas. Actually, Tom brought an unusual combination of skills and experiences to our project because he was both a professional actor and a professional designer. His history is interesting and relevant to how we all had instant rapport on this adventure:

"I studied art and architecture in school," Tom says. "I thought I would either be an artist or, perhaps, an architect. Then I got bitten by the acting bug and was an actor for twenty-five years. All along, through my acting career, the love of architecture and interior design was literally my second love. I never gave up on it as my other passion. Even though I never attempted to make a living with it, I was always dealing with it. Many of my friends saw what I would do for myself and would ask me to help them out with one of their projects. For ten, fifteen, twenty years I did that for fun, and many of those people became celebrities and would be asked who was their designer. So for twenty years the phone rang time and time again asking me to do this, but I always said, 'No, that's not what I'm trying to do.'

"Then, one day I became a father and someone called one morning about nine o'clock and, as an out-of-work actor, I was just starting my day. This friend called to tell me about a writer friend who wanted work done on her house. I said, 'Thanks, but no thanks. It's not what I want to do.' Two weeks later I woke up about that same time and realized the phone hadn't rung with acting jobs. I thought to myself, 'Why am I constantly pursuing this door that occasionally opens when this other door constantly is being knocked on and I don't open it. It's just being ridiculous.'

"Maybe it was the sense of responsibility of having a new baby in the next room, but I called my friend back, met with the client, and it was a wonderful experience. Soon, it was as if there was something in the universe that told everybody 'Calloway is doing this work now,' because, instantly, all kinds of work started coming to me."

So after finding Marty, and then a year or so later coming across Tom, I asked these two strangers to work together. Ignorance of the laws of how things get done is not a defense, and when I introduced the idea of using Marty to Tom, he tried to explain to us, "Well, I really have my own people and there's kind of a shorthand I use with my own people." He clearly wasn't enthused about working with an unknown contractor. I urged him, "I know, but you'll like Marty. Why don't you guys meet?"

Finally, he said, "Okay, yeah, I'll meet with him."

Tom would later say that he was unsure at the time, but it couldn't have worked out better because he got a contractor who he thinks is the greatest, but it *is* a backward way of doing it.

"It did take us a little longer," Tom says, "because we had to establish a language from us to communicate what we both wanted. That made it difficult because Marty wasn't thinking about the historical details and the minutiae which makes it different from something that's just been built and something that's been there all along. He wasn't used to building with that point of view. So the numbers—the bids—he gave Rick and Tudi were based on a much simpler kind of cut-and-dried way of doing things. He would give a bid for the pool table room, which is a very different experience than any room you would walk into on a daily basis. That

> Humor is emotional chaos remembered in tranquility.
> — James Thurber

kind of woodwork, the details, those kinds of doors and beams—all that stuff—he wasn't bidding on that on day one. He gave them numbers based on what he *thought* it was going to be, and the house hadn't been designed yet, let alone by someone whose coming from the point of view that I'm coming from.

"But the actual working with Marty couldn't have been better, and I've been using him regularly ever since. We're on our third or fourth project together and I just think the world of him and I wouldn't have known him if they hadn't brought us together."

So I took a chance with Tom and Marty and it worked out. Mainly, what we liked about Tom was that he had a pleasing way of creating a living environment. He takes his time and knows that everybody's tastes are a little different. If he really felt strongly about something, he would fight for it. Like the antique glass in the ceiling window over the kitchen island that I wanted instead of the wired safety glass Tom had in mind. So he was good that way, and besides, didn't somebody once say that a difference of opinion is what makes horse races and missionaries? I think it was Mark Twain.

Tom wasn't really sure what he was getting into even as he was getting into it, but he said, "If you're going to bring me on, I want to do this whole thing, this whole look."

I said sure, but that's not really the way it finally turned out. Tudi and I were very active participants in the entire remodeling and had a lot to say about the final look. The big thing that Tom gave us was perspective—a concept of the totality of our new home. In essence, he ran the whole project backward in our minds—like reversing the drive on a movie—so we thought about the end before we thought about the beginning. He wanted us to decide where we were going to go, before we started our journey.

Instead of our focusing on a wall here and a window there, Tom made us start thinking in terms of a cohesive overall picture. The phrase that kept running through our minds about the existing style of the house was "hodgepodge" in that it lacked a theme.

At the beginning, when Tom came over to see us he said, "Wow, this is a great house."

Flattered, I'm thinking, "Yeah, we did really good. We found a house that had all the things we wanted."

He looked at it and said, "There's not a real style here." Of course, the house had been redone four or five times since it was first built in 1949.

He said, "I'm seeing a Spanish Mediterranean feel."

I reacted, saying, "Yeah, I'm right there with you! I absolutely—"

"Perhaps with a Spanish tile roof."

Tudi was heard from on that idea instantly: "No!" There she was, being wishy-washy again. "I'm scared of Spanish tile roofs. The tile is too heavy and this is earthquake country."

This, of course, proved how much the Californiazation of Tudi had progressed, because she now understood that there are four seasons in Southern California:

Summer:	hot, earthquakes
Fall:	wildfires, earthquakes
Winter:	rains, earthquakes
Spring:	mud slides, earthquakes

Tom soothed the moment, "Well, perhaps we could find a nice light, composition tile for the roof. We could make this look really nice."

I'm going, "Yes! I think you're right."

Tom said, "Also, I would like to create a larger entryway."

"What would we have to do?"

"We really wouldn't have to do much because there's noth-ing above it." (I would later learn that "we never had to do much" always cost money. But I digress.)

Tom continued, "All we have to do is go up. Then, you have a grander entrance so you're not walking into an eight- or nine-foot ceiling. You're walking into something that's going up with maybe a chandelier and some lights."

"Yeah, that's great."

"Then, I'm looking at the house and I'm seeing all different kinds of windows. . . . Some are metal, some are wood, some are plastic, and some are not plastic."

"Yeah, I know."

We began to understand this line of thinking of Tom's, which was incremental because everything is interrelated to each other and changing one part of the house would require other changes in other places.

This conceptualizing may be why Tom is so much in demand as a designer, although we didn't know just how much he was sought after at the beginning. (For example, we had no idea that he might be doing Pat Riley's house in Miami one day and doing ours the next.) We just knew he was a friend of Mike Farrell and Shelly Fabre and that we liked what he'd done with their place. It's really nice. Mike and Shelly bought the "Mr. Ed" house, or rather the house owned by Alan Young, who owned the horse "Mr. Ed" from the TV show of the same name. We could make a lot of horse jokes about that, but the point was that Mike and Shelly bought the horse house and remodeled it with Tom's help and he did a great job on it.

When Tom brought up the jumble of window styles, I began to realize this was much bigger than I expected. The windows may well have been my Rubicon leading to bigger, better, and scarier remodeling. Sometimes one passes a turning point without realizing it, like picking the wrong tie for that important job interview. Unthinkingly, I was starting to tip over dominoes where one decision triggers another and another—particularly when it came to the more expansive and expensive decisions we were about to make on this house. It began with the windows, and that led to the stucco that led to the roof that led to who knows what else? My initial feelings as to what would be easy and done within three months were beginning to evaporate.

At one point I thought about asking my dad to come down to Los Angeles and supervise the whole remodeling project. In some ways that made sense to me, since he was alone now that my mother had passed away from cancer and it would give him something to do while giving us the benefit of his experience and know-how. In the end, we all decided it probably wouldn't work because he was retired and L.A. was a different construction environment with different building codes, but he would occasionally visit.

Dad must've thought it was ironic that I was massively involved in this remodeling project at all. I mean, I hadn't shown the inclination toward the building profession. There were a few times when he had me nailing floors or roofs, but it was very clear to him that I was going in a different direction. But somewhere along the line, I drifted back. Maybe it was owning a home of my own that triggered it. Because now I could clearly see how Dad could spend months working on projects or building drawings, such as the plans for the new Pine Lake summerhouse. I'd come home from school and he'd show them to me, and I was really interested as he carefully explained the reasoning to me: "Yeah, see that? I got the stairs here that'll get up to the second floor, and under the stairs around here and here out by the kitchen there's storage space for shelves . . . " The next day I'd come in and he'd go, "Nah, I changed the stairs. You know, I've got this over here . . . "

He would change it and go back and forth, noodling for a long time, getting it exactly the way he wanted it. However, he complicated matters by coming across things in his construction work like a door or a cabinet nobody wanted. He stored this stuff in the garage and had to keep changing the plans to fit the new item he'd acquired. Now I was doing the same thing Dad had done: constantly reassessing the plans and looking for new ideas. Had I become my father after all? All of a sudden, three months went by with conversations, meetings, and basic plans drawn, and we hadn't even gotten the building permits yet. How could this be? Why did it take so long?

Somebody once cautioned me against impatience. He said time was God's way of keeping everything from happening all at once. Well, okay, but the waiting was getting frustrating.

It turned out that the waiting was the easy part.

Remodeling the Mansion Without Remodeling the Marriage

Fortunately for me, besides "I love you," the three words my wife loves me to say more than any other are "I'll fix it." Even so, I couldn't always say that, and sometimes there were so many delays waiting for the delivery of materials and the arrival of workmen, I felt like I was on stage waiting for Godot.

What is rarely talked about in remodeling is *stress*. Remodeling is emotionally stressful, as designers, contractors, architects, and psychologists will tell you if you probe them deeply enough. It is actually called "Remodeling Stress Syndrome" or RSS. A classic example we heard of was a licensed family counselor in Santa Barbara who went through a remodeling project. She said that it left her completely strung out and stressed, and she's a pro at handling tension.

The concern here is that the anxiety of remodeling can put destructive pressure on a personal relationship or marriage, with the result that the home is a dream and the marriage is a nightmare. Some of the things that couples might think of doing to ease the burden on their relationship are to sort out possible conflict points before you begin, whether they be tensions related to the relationship, the remodeling, or both. For example, if you're tense over relatives, you should settle that before trying to settle on the tile in the bathroom. You should talk about and agree on what your goal is as to the final look and feel of the remodeled home: colors, materials, and so on. It's often smart to talk about your general concepts separately with the designer at the beginning so you each can talk without interruption or open conflict. Let the designer help mediate differences, and later, when you get to the details, the designer can offer the couple alternatives, with the cost of each.

Understand the process of remodeling, and that it will disrupt your life for longer than you think and will cost more than you planned. If you're not prepared to have workmen in the house at seven A.M. watching you brush your teeth while they mount wallboard, you're going to be an unhappy remodeler. In which case, you should try to stay somewhere else during the process, as we did. Also, if you're worried about precious things getting broken during the remodeling, pack them up and put them in storage. It's worth the cost to avoid the aggravation.

Finally, think about your own personality type and how it will react to what goes on during a remodeling. If, for example, you are obsessive-compulsive, you'll probably be climbing the walls during construction because materials (and men) don't always arrive on time, nor are they installed as you might want them. And they also cost more than you planned, which can ratchet up the tension. As I look back, I think in some ways my training as a professional actor was helpful. By playing different roles, it gives me the ability to see different people's viewpoints in a particular situation. Such as how the contractor, the designer, the electrician, and my wife all view a simple plug. Ironically, my first role in school was in the play *Comedy of Errors*, which is prophetic, given the subject of this book.

Tom has done many remodels and has to work with many couples, and the dynamics of that came as a surprise to him when he first got into the designer profession:

"The most remarkable thing to me about this profession is the number of hats I have to wear. The intimacy that you have with your clients is enormous. You become a part of the family and you witness every disagreement between the couples." Rick and Tudi were an exception because they were very much of a like mind, "but, in most cases it is very common for husbands and wives to have absolutely opposing views. It's remarkable how many people get together and stay together who have completely separate points of view. I am constantly in the middle trying to massage the situation so that they'll end up happy; so one person isn't negating what we really should do while the other person is screaming the silent scream."

Some of Tom's tips:

"Going into this process, if one doesn't have to live in the house while it's being remodeled, not sleep there—that's a huge help. Sometimes the work isn't actually slow, but it seems so when you're put through the daily misery of living there.

"Second, it's really important to find someone you are compatible with as a designer. It's important to find the person who's going to help you get what you want or help lead you to what you may not even know you want, so when you're done, you feel it's what you want. That's key.

"Of course, it's going to take twice as long as you ever dreamed and cost at least twice as much. The more you can plan in advance and put it on paper and feel clear about it, the less money it's going to cost you in changes later on. But there's no project, no matter how well-planned, that people don't get better ideas or new ideas along the way—particularly in a remodel—that leads you in different directions. You have to keep yourself open to those changes or you'll become very unhappy."

Tudi and I took turns being angry

> I guess one of the truths we learned is a marriage and a home are a lot alike. No matter how long it's been around, there is always work to do on it.

and frustrated—which helped us make it through. One thing neither of us could possibly imagine was living in the house while it was being remodeled. One friend who went through this said, "Do you know what it means to come home to a neat house where everything works, where everything is the right color and the lady of the house is happy? It means you're in the wrong house."

At times, what held our marriage together was Tudi being big enough to step back, take a deep breath, and see where I was wrong.

Time Lapse and Brain Lapse

In many ways, the mental and physical processes of remodeling are separate and different. It is like being an oarsman in a rowing crew where the boat is going in one direction while almost everyone is looking in another direction. There are two kinds of lapses during remodeling: the time lapse and the brain lapse. With the time lapse, I made decisions about things I didn't see completed until weeks later, and then they were sometimes done differently than what we had in mind.

The brain lapse was an affliction of the workman who didn't think about the end result of his work. For example, I accidentally came upon an electrician installing a cumbersome switch panel in the open wall between the kitchen and the laundry room facing the kitchen. I asked him to reverse it to face into the laundry room where it couldn't be seen. He couldn't understand that the industrial-looking electrical plate was ugly and, as he explained to me, our adding extra lights in the den required a bigger electrical panel. I said that was fine but the panel could still be open into the laundry room and out of sight. He looked at me and, without a hint of irony, said "That's a great idea."

At the same time, I took a closer look at him, remembering my dad warned me never to hire an electrician with singed eyebrows.

In another incident, I was playing the AT&T Golf Open at Pebble Beach when I saw these wonderful copper gutters and downspouts at my hotel. Instantly, I knew there was no other way to go. The copper added a tone better than anything else could have. So when I got back to our dream house, that became Change Order #30. When the gutters and downspouts were installed, we ran into another typical brain lapse that happens so often in remodeling.

The idea of downspouts is to carry water from the roof away from where we walked, but the workmen set them to empty onto the concrete walks so we would slosh through the water. I wanted them to drain into flower beds and soak into the ground. When I explained that to the workmen, they were amazed and thought it a clever idea.

Part of our remodeling problems came from these brain lapses and time lapses. This is exacerbated by the changes in the construction industry since I was a kid, and the remodeling job drove the point home. One major change was the "Ship Last Minute" mentality that keeps retailers from stocking furniture, carpeting, etc. because it ties up their capital. So the industry now orders an item at the last minute—only after a customer orders it—and only then does the manufacturer make and ship it. This stretches out remodeling jobs and makes them more aggravating and expensive.

> Nobody will accept responsibility for any mistakes on a construction project until they have exhausted every other possibility, including El Niño.

The contractor would ask, "Do you want this, or this?"

And I'd say, "I want that."

A few days later he'd come back and say, "You can't have it."

"Then why did you offer it to me?"

"The factory's on the East Coast and they're back-ordered four months." It's standard for all factories to be on the opposite coast from where you are, and everything in the universe is "back-ordered four months." I'm confident that, when Captain Kirk first ordered the starship *Enterprise*, he was told it's back-ordered two eons.

"Then, let's start over," I'd say, and they brought me the next choice. I'm not picky, I just wanted to know what we could do and move on to the next item.

Bill Gates is the richest man in the world because of a program called Windows 95. I could have become the poorest man in America because of a program called Windows 96.

Early in the remodeling, replacing the windows became a major point if we were going to get a cohesive style, and if the house was going to decide what it was going to be when it grew up. We'd already agreed on the basic remodeling and work was progressing on that when Tom, Marty, Tudi, and I finally focused on the window changes. The significance of this decision is marked by the fact that changing the windows became Change Order #1 and it was the single most expensive of all the other 101 (Yes, that's one hundred and one—it's not a typo) Change Orders that would follow. The changing of the windows, unbeknownst to me, would affect everything else we were planning.

As we talked about windows, Marty's men were going ahead with Tom's marvelous idea about raising the ceiling over the entry to the house. Then, one day, we heard a yell from the living room: "Wow, look at this!" They had broken through the plaster wall to raise the roof of the entry hall and discovered the roof was held up by inadequate supports. A major reinforcement was necessary to keep the roof from collapsing. I asked Tom what it would take to save it. He answered: "Money."

This was a cartoon moment for me. You know, when the little lightbulb goes on over your head in a moment of clarity and recognition. This would be the first of many unexpected discoveries as we went through the remodeling, and as we later

Historic Building Blunders

Galloping Gertie

My roof was nothing compared to the flawed construction design of the Tacoma Narrows Bridge (Tacoma, Washington) over Puget Sound, near where I was born eighteen years later. From the day it opened on July 1, 1940, the bridge was nicknamed Galloping Gertie because it undulated in the wind. It would wave up and down so much that motorists would lose sight of cars in front of and behind them. Some car passengers complained about getting seasick on the bridge.

On November 7, 1940, a 42-mph wind whipped across the bridge, causing it to undulate so badly they closed it to traffic with several vehicles trapped on the bridge. The occupants abandoned their vehicles but were unable to stand up on the waving bridge. They had to crawl on their hands and knees to safety as the bridge literally danced itself to destruction. The only fatality was a cocker spaniel mistakenly left behind in one of the abandoned cars.

learned, it's common with remodel jobs. It was the point when I realized that some construction work had been done on this house over the years without permits or inspections. As one uncovers a wall or floor or whatever, there is revealed the sins of previous workers who bootlegged changes to the building.

Even so, I wondered how come the people before me didn't have to get legitimate building permits and clearances like I'd had to do? Was I the only one following the rules? How did other homes get built?

And something else was happening: the "What If" factor. All of a sudden, as things are being taken apart and remolded, your mind lets loose an enzyme in your brain that I call the "What If" enzyme. All of a sudden, because this wall is being redone, it's like, "What If?" and Pandora's box springs open. What if? What if we change THE ENTIRE HOUSE?

For example, in the kitchen where we were only going to change the tile, the "what ifs" resulted in all new appliances including two microwaves, cabinets being stained (twice because of error), antique glass cabinet doors, hard-to-find special pull knobs, a wine and spice rack (both done wrong), and, our favorite Change Order, a tumbled marble floor. All of that probably started with, "Well, 'what if' you raised this kitchen ceiling?"

Seemed like a good idea, and so the workmen went into the kitchen and opened it up with some decorative beams across. Once they opened it up and saw there was another one or one and a half feet above it, Tom said, "You have the space. Why don't we raise the ceiling in the kitchen too?"

We hadn't been planning on it, but decided to do it. Same thing happened in the living room. We were going to put some beams in, and again they looked and said, "Well, you've got room up there. Why don't we go up?"

Obviously, high ceilings open up the room a little more. So we raised quite a few ceilings: the dining room, the kitchen, the living room, entryway, and the master bedroom, which was the only ceiling we wanted to raise originally.

Then I was back thinking about that major decision over the windows. Since it was important, I asked my dad, who, I must say, was very delicate in his comments about our remodeling when he would come to visit. He saw that I was passionate about our plans, and he didn't want to pooh-pooh too many of my ideas. Still, he wondered why I was changing all those windows. "They're perfectly good windows," he said as we stood on the lawn.

"I know but, Dad, there's a lot of different types of windows and we're trying to . . . " I'm tap-dancing at this point. "I'm trying to create a style . . . You know . . . we're trying to go with a . . . "

I'm pleading to his architectural sensibilities that we're going to make a cohesive style out of this house. He wasn't taking the bait. "They're perfectly good windows," he repeated. "You paid a lot of money for that house, and do you really want to spend that much more money just so the windows look the same?"

"Well, yes. I do. And, I *can!* It's my house."

Dad shrugged, and so I knew I was on my own.

I knew they were perfectly good windows, including two or three really beautiful bay windows. The dining room and kitchen had full plate windows that I really liked because I could look through the window and it was easy on the eyes. But I decided to change all the other windows.

Now, did we want divided windows or undivided windows? Tom said you couldn't have nondivided windows next to divided windows. Besides, he explained, the classical style that we wanted was divided windows, and Tudi agreed. I, on the other hand, was reluctant to give up the big picture windows in the dining room and kitchen because they were so pretty. I'm still not sure why you can't have divided and nondivided windows next to each other. Who made up that rule? Was it Lincoln who said, "I can't stand a house with windows divided against itself?" I don't think so. Anyhow, I have since seen many homes built in the 1920s and 1930s in Spanish Mediterranean styles that had picture windows.

There are a lot of decisions like this when you're remodeling, and you end up compromising and learning to live with the consequences. I did it. But I will say that I still miss looking through a window without any dividers to it. On the other hand, as I look at it now, it's nice and cohesive. So, there's Style vs. Function.

At this point the windows were out and we were ready to put a light composite tile on the roof. If you think about that last sentence, you may ask how the two separate elements—windows and light composite tile roof—are connected, and why are they in the same sentence? Though seemingly unrelated, the two are intertwined, as you will see in a moment, and it's a very important point about remodeling. So hang with me for a minute on this.

We found a local company that made beautiful wood windows and we ordered them.

Then, all of a sudden, Tom said in his straightforward way, "We can't use those windows."

"What do you mean?" I asked, my mind racing for an instant solution.

"Well, upstairs the double-hung windows aren't big enough for firemen to get out."

"Firemen don't have to get out of our house. No firemen live here," I answered.

"No, no. They have to be able to climb in or out."

"Oh, well, what if I leave the windows that are in now?"

"Well, if we stay with the size of the windows that are up there now, they won't meet the current building code."

This was a classic lose-lose situation, and I had the miracle of building codes to thank for it.

A Word About Building Codes

There are certain things that go on in the building of a house that are code and have some related history lesson attached to them. For example, there are some people who want to tear down a house completely, but they can't do it totally. They have to leave an existing wall—a "grandfathered-in" wall—standing so they can meet the charade of it not being a complete demolition to be replaced with all new construction. If it is all new construction, it has to meet the standards of new building codes, but if it's "only a remodeling of an existing structure"—that single wall—it can be done under the old, less stringent building code.

Suppose, for example, the old wall was only three feet from the property line and the new building code forbids having a structure any closer than ten feet from the property line. If they took that old wall out, they wouldn't be able to build in that space because it's too close to the property line. But since the wall is already there, you can leave that wall and build onto it. For reasons only known to the building industry and God, the building code for remodeling is not as strict as if you are building new from scratch.

So there are loopholes and ways of getting around some building code restrictions, but building codes are often good for the home owner's safety. It's just that they take some strange turns at times. For example, in my house during the remodeling we had to obey the *new* building codes even when we were changing things built under the old building code. Or we would discover work done by a previous owner that was bootlegged, that is, it was done without getting a proper building permit. There were noncode aluminum gas lines under the house which, if they leaked, could have led to an explosion, fire, or suffocation of all of us. I was happy to

Historic Building Blunders

Popping Glass Windows

I n 1972 the John Hancock Tower became famous for windows popping out and falling to the ground. As a result, the building stood empty for four years, streets below it were closed, and it became known as the "plywood palace" for all the boarded-up windows. The correction of the popping windows *doubled* the final $95 million cost of the building, making it one of the most expensive construction disasters in history. The cause: flaws in the building frame and foundation.

see the entire system replaced with steel pipe as required by the building code.

There is also a strange code in California that says the first light to come on in a kitchen or bathroom must be fluorescent. Since fluorescent light is harsh and flat, most women hate having it in the bathroom. So what often happens is home owners and builders install the fluorescent fixture until the building inspector has approved the job. Then, they disconnect or remove it.

Another example on the federal level is the passage of a law by Congress in 1992, the Energy Policy and Conservation

Act, that makes it illegal to install 3.5-gallon toilets in homes. It calls for 1.6-gallon toilets instead. The idea, apparently, is to save water, but like so many do-gooder ideas passed into law by legislative bodies, the general public doesn't like it. So, guess what? Canadians are doing a big business smuggling 3.5-gallon toilets across the border into the U.S. in a modern-day version of Prohibition.

So there are things that have to be done because of code, and apparently, in this case, the windows in the upstairs of the house were in flagrant violation of the firemen's code, but since they were already there, they could stay. But if we were going to remove them, we had to have something bigger and different.

I immediately looked on the bright side. This was one more justification for changing these "perfectly good windows." I could tell my dad they were in flagrant violation of firemen's bodies. So we had to substitute crank-out windows in lieu of the double-hung. I wondered if our windows had to accommodate *all* firemen, because didn't they come in small, medium, and large like everyone else? Or maybe the new code only said "average" firemen's bodies, and if so, how can you tell? Does the fire department keep two or three "average" firemen on call so they can go around to remodeling jobs and test the windows by crawling in and out of them? Or maybe this whole thing was a hoax lobbied through the city by the burglars' union?

The new windows came from a wonderful little company just outside downtown Los Angeles and were wood with white weather-stripping that you didn't notice because the windows were a natural wood color. It never even crossed my mind that there was weather-stripping on them. We painted them with primer—white primer—because we knew were going to finish-paint them with another coat later on and we never noticed that white weather-stripping—not until we had the windows painted. All of a sudden we had blue-green windows with white weather-stripping all the way around and through the middle.

I was totally alarmed.

"Oh, no. Wait a minute! What happened? Wha . . . wha . . . Can we change the weather-stripping?"

"No, we could have gotten it in black or dark brown," Marty said.

"Well, why didn't we get it in dark brown?"

"Well, we didn't know we were going to paint the windows this color."

"Oh, man."

So there went hundreds of dollars more for labor to change the weather-stripping. I have since seen it in white at a hotel in the town of Ojai (another of those California Spanish words, pronounced, "Oh-hi") and it looked alright. This was another remodeling lesson: Sometimes it's better to live with something for a while rather then go with the knee-jerk response. If you have a lot of money, you can afford a lot of knee-jerk responses. If you have a lot of money and a lot of common sense, you can cut those knee-jerk responses in half.

We're very family oriented, as evidenced by our families' interest in the remodeling. We enjoyed it when our relatives from Washington and Texas would drop by to see how things were going even if we didn't always agree on the project.

When my dad, Gene, came to see how things were going after we had taken out the old windows, he said, "So, I see you replaced the windows," as if he were thinking out loud.

"Yeah, well, you knew I was going to do that."

"Yeah, I know, I know," he said, and

> Good judgment comes from experience and a lot of that comes from bad judgment.

shook his head as if to say, "I hope he knows what he's doing."

I could see that he still couldn't understand why I'd done it. They weren't broken. They weren't warped. And there were forty-eight of them. Only forty-eight?

Plus we put in French doors everywhere to add to the sense of coherence. We added them in the master bedroom, the pool table room, the media room, and in the den. And, in all the ceiling raising, we were adding a new roof. My dad noticed that too.

"And the roof," he added when he saw that the old roof was stripped away and the house frame was open to the sky.

"Yeah," I said carefully. At that point I didn't have the

Historic Building Blunders

The Tower of Pisa

A classic case is the famous Leaning Tower of Pisa that was begun in 1174 by the architect Bonanno Pisano as part of a city square called the Field of Miracles that also contained an exquisite cathedral. The tower was built without careful investigation of the soil on which it would stand. This was mud and compressible clay and sand for about thirty-three feet. Below that was a layer of hard and compressible clay along with sand for another thirty-four feet, and under that it was sand saturated with water. So from the outset the tower was not a building that would rest on bedrock as it should have. As a result, the tower has leaned from the very beginning. It

heart to tell him we were putting on that expensive Spanish tile roof too.

"You know you should get a tarp up there on that roof."

"Well, it's Southern California and it doesn't rain that much." Even so, Marty put a tarp up over the roof frame.

Three days later it was still California but it was also pouring buckets of rain. But, of course, some strong winds ripped part of the tarp off and the rain soaked parts of the house. The media room's ceiling collapsed and Marty had to completely redo it. The only way I could look at it was, "It could have been worse." And thank God for dads.

began tilting from the first day of construction, but the building went ahead anyhow as they wedged mortar under the one side to stop the leaning. This worked, except it shifted to tilting toward the other side. The construction was stopped three terraces up and stood that way for almost a century because of warfare between Pisa and other Italian cities. When construction resumed in 1272, the tower was completed but continued to lean, and in the course of time became famous. In the earlier days, the engineers didn't have the tools with which to shore up this tower built on unstable soil. Now they do have the engineering solution but are faced with the more difficult obstacle of the politicians of Pisa. The local politicians don't want the tower closed so corrective work can be done because it brings in $2 million tourist-dollars a year. Besides, as one observer noted, who would travel to Italy to see the Straight Tower of Pisa?

We were then into November–December. Originally, we were going to be done in August with our little remodeling project. It was now nearly winter and we hadn't touched what we were going to do in the first place.

Tudi observed my father when he came to visit. "Gene was interesting to watch," she said. "He just kind of strolled around and nodded his head and then we would say, 'Well, we're getting rid of this.' Then he'd say, 'Well, why are you going to do that? That works just fine.' My parents would do the same thing. Obviously, their generation grew up not just in a different time, but in a different mind-set. In my parents' day and when Gene was building, everything was less expensive. He built the house Rick grew up in for $9,000, the whole house. Our kitchen floor cost more than that.

"My mother came to visit right after we bought the house, and I took a video of her touring the place before we did anything. She was interested in everything and loved some things, such as the decorative tile in the kitchen with pictures on it. Mom said, 'Oh, what a cute cow! You're not going to get rid of the cow tile are you?'

"'Mom, the cow is history,' I told her. 'We're getting rid of this kitchen. I want new tile.'

"She couldn't understand why we were getting rid of the cow. So I had the contractor take it out and put it in the garage to give to her for Christmas. Still haven't done it, but there are more Christmases coming. I probably will wrap it up as a joke, but I suspect she'll want to keep it because she loves that cow. Actually, the cow is really a bull, as our friend, Joyce pointed out later, but Mom and I started out thinking it was a cow.

"Then, between the dining room and the pool table room, was a leaded glass window. We were going to remove it, and she said, 'Oh, you're getting rid of that? It's so beautiful.' At that point I didn't have the heart to tell her we were also replacing the leaded glass front door. She would know soon enough. We tried to dole out the disappointments slowly to our parents.

"The point of this is that our parents would ask, 'Why waste this when it's perfectly good?' I grew up that way and actually would agree, but once we started and we were going for it, neither Rick nor I wanted to settle. If we're going to do this, let's do it right. Thus, it became 'the money pit.'"

Spackle and Hide

The windows were in, and this is the point when Marty, our contractor, said reluctantly, "As hard as we try to patch the stucco around the windows, it's always going to look like patchwork."

"Uh-oh, so, what are you telling me? The stucco will look like patchwork and there's nothing we can do?" I braced myself.

"I think you'd be better off to restucco the whole thing."

"When I brought up the idea of new windows, you thought it was a good idea but you didn't tell me about the stucco?" I immediately had mixed feelings. This was a real turning point.

"Yeah," he answered, as if it were the most sensible thing in the world.

Then, I asked the inevitable question: "How much is that going to be?"

"I'll write you up a bid."

The bid came in and I could feel the blood drain out of my face as my complexion probably turned the color of the stucco that was being proposed for such an enormous additional cost. But in time my heart started pumping again and, as it did, I thought about how nice it would look and how this was a good thing because, now, I could get the kind of stucco I wanted. By now I realized I could trick myself into seeing the good in any catastrophe.

So all the old stucco came down and I had a house with no windows in it, no stucco on it, and they hadn't even gotten to the bedroom and the kitchen, which, if you remember, were all we were going to do in the first place.

So the change in the windows led to the change in the stucco, and now we finally come to how that, in turn, led to the change in the roof. The roof, as Tom pointed out, was a major part of the visual presentation of the house, and we could either try to ignore it or we could acknowledge it. If we acknowledged the presence of the roof—and it is hard not to— Tom wanted it to flow into the style of Spanish Mediterranean we were aiming at, and that meant ceramic red Spanish tile. Tudi nixed that because of her fear that it would be too heavy and too dangerous in earthquake territory where we now lived.

To recap: you will recall that we were going to go with a Spanish-tile-looking composition shingle. But that was BW–BS: Before Windows–Before Stucco. Now came one of the big Change Orders: the roof. Marty took me aside and said, "I wasn't going to say this before because, at the time, you weren't going to take the stucco off. But now that we have the stucco off, you know, we could put up ¾-inch plywood, strengthen those walls, and you could put a real tile roof on."

We held up a real Spanish tile next to the composite tile we had planned on using. The composite tile had a tract-house look to it while the real Spanish tile was rich and right. There was no question about the difference in quality.

How Much?

"Let me write you up a bid."

So, one small step for mankind and one giant leap for the checkbook.

With the new reinforced walls in the house, we were ready for the new Spanish tile roof and for the new stucco on the outside of the house to give it a

> Remodeling can be a religious experience — you need faith to get through it.

special "Spanish Mediterranean look." I could see this "Spanish look" clearly in my head, but getting it out of my head and into the minds of my wife, the contractor, and the designer was not easy. You can tell somebody, "I want you to stucco this wall," but that's not enough.

Believe me, I actually drove around looking at houses, and almost every house in California has stucco, but every stucco is different. There's a different swirl here, a different touch there, a different material elsewhere—it was mind-boggling. What I pictured was a Spanish Mediterranean, but I wanted the stucco to be more Mediterranean than Spanish. What did that mean? It didn't mean anything to anybody except to me. It meant I wanted a light Mediterranean stucco that looked like you're thirty feet away when you're two feet in front of it. From thirty feet away, there was not a blemish, not a trowel mark—NOTHING. Nice, undulating, white stucco with the Mediterranean Sea in the background. This is what I was imagining. Now, the reality was, it would look like that from thirty feet away, but when you got up to it, it wouldn't. So I had to find a compromise. And before I could find a compromise, I had to find the right words to tell the man who was doing the stucco what I wanted.

Images in your mind are very strong, very persuading. Everything in your mind is perfect. Everything that pops into your mind is *done!* And, it looks great! But in fact, it has to get done, and somebody, who is not you, has to make it look like what's in your mind. Let me say at this point that it's very helpful to find pictures that are close enough to the picture in your mind that you can show somebody. You can tell somebody, "I want this or I want that," but it's not enough. Tudi tried to help by going to the library, bringing home pictures and also driving around looking at stucco walls.

She asked me, "What do you want?"

Historic Building Blunders
Falling Walls

Walls falling off buildings are much more common than most people know. Oftentimes, a failed facade will be detected and repaired before it actually falls off and endangers people below. Sometimes the failed facade is discovered too late, as with the State Office Building in Hauppauge, New York (1977), where an entire window wall peeled away from the building and crashed to the street. At the University of Massachusetts, bricks have been falling from the twenty-eight-story library building in Amherst for seven years while students enter the building through tunnels.

"Well, I want it smooth, but wavy."

Then she would bring in a picture she'd found and I'd say, "No, that's lumpy."

"Okay, so not lumpy but smooth and, yet, wavy."

So she picked another picture, and I told her, "No, that's grainy. That's got the sand in it."

"Okay, so I understand that, no sand."

Tudi felt my search was really important and was trying to find the answer. She spent hours at the bookstore, looking at photographs. One day she came home and said, "Rick, I was driving around over in so-and-so and I saw this wall and I think it might be what you mean. Come on."

So we got in the car and went to look at those people's wall.

"Well, that's almost right, but not really," I said.

I just wanted to find *the* wall to take the contractor or the stucco guy to see and say, "Do this." We never really found it, but we muddled through, and I think they accomplished it. But it was hard getting there. It was very time- and thought-consuming. I finally came up with the word *after* the stucco was done: *buttery*.

What is *buttery?* It's if you try to make a block of butter smooth and it's still wavy.

Of course, that was after the fact, but you'll find when you're remodeling your house, a lot of things happen after the fact, and at least we did not have some of the problems that happened on other construction jobs where the walls fell down.

Even so, they did a great job with my floundering suggestions and got, basically, not what I envisioned, but what I should have. And, I'm happy. But if I'd had that one adjective, it would have made things so much easier.

Words and Visitors

The Magic Word That Makes It Possible

One thing that helped us through all this was that Tudi and I took turns getting upset. That really was good because, if we were both upset at the same time, it would have been devastating. Then we would have both been moping around and nothing would have gotten done. So we took turns, and that was helpful because sometimes the problem was missed communications among us, the designer, or the contractor. For example, three-quarters of the way in we're thinking, "Okay, we've got to cut back. Everything is costing a lot more than we anticipated." Like couples everywhere caught up in the remodeling whirlwind, we thought we might have to cut back on a few little things—like food and clothing.

An example of how difficult this was is the master bedroom cabinet episode. We had this area in the master bathroom where we wanted to put a nice cabinet. We also had space behind the bedroom door where we decided to put a cabinet as well. We got the bids for the two different cabinets and it was very expensive and we thought, "Okay, I don't mind spending the money in the master bathroom, where I'll see it more often, but behind the bedroom door we could just go with a regular paint grade cabinet and cut costs there." When Tudi relayed the message to Marty, she thought I meant the reverse. When Marty talked to both of us, we were both saying exactly the opposite thing and he finally had to come to both of us at the same time and say, "Okay, explain to me what you want." It was frustrating, and another example of the need for clear communications in remodeling.

One of the things I marveled at with Tudi was her patience while we were trying to solve some of the problems of mix-ups.

Some days it seemed that all we were accomplishing was gathering material for a future TV situation comedy.

One unclear communication began early, between Tom and me. I told him that, because I'm on *Home Improvement*, there's the possibility I might be able to get certain things at a discount. This would not benefit Tom because the designer gets a percentage of whatever he buys for you. I tried to make him aware of the fact that he might not be buying and getting commissions on as much materials as he might normally get. His reaction was a kind of uncomprehending disbelief: "Oh, yeah, okay. Sure." He didn't realize that because of the work I do on *Home Improvement*, certain perks and opportunities presented themselves. And I don't know when or where or what, but the last six years have taught me that it happens.

Marty understood this. "Rick has had some real good fortune," he said of me. "He had some misfortune, but a lot of good fortune, too. He's a deal maker. I couldn't believe him. He would come back from a trade show with thousands of dollars worth of stuff. There was, for example, all that molding and baseboard that Rick bought from the Canadian lumber people."

(I met them at an Orchard How-To Fair. the supply all the moldings and baseboards for Orchard Supply Hardware. I asked them if they would give me a bid on the moldings and baseboards for the house, and they said, "Sure, send us the specifications." So I sent them the specifications, not knowing they weren't really set up to do the kind of work I wanted, but they DID IT!)

"So," Marty said, "Tom drew up the design of what the detail would look like and sent that to them. They made the knives for that design and put them on their machines and zipped the molds off in no time. They crated it all up, and one day this huge eighteen-wheeler came with these huge crates with all this molding, and it came all the way from Canada."

The power of Al. And the bid they gave us came in at about half the original bid.

"They were delighted to do it, and I guess Rick's picture is still hanging in their office."

Another cost-saving opportunity came from the folks at Glidden Paints. At the time, I was representing Liquid Nails, a subsidiary of theirs, when they mentioned to me they had a wonderful paint product suitable for Southern California living. It's called ELAS-AMERIC and has the ability to move with the house when small seismic shifts (Point 3 or smaller) happen without cracking. In addition, they were able to match the blue-gray-green ice plant color Tudi wanted. She spotted the color one day when she, Tom, and I were looking at paint jobs on other homes. At one home, we didn't like the painting, but Tudi looked down and exclaimed, "That's it! That's the color I want." It took us a moment to realize she was talking about the ice plant near where we were standing. And that's the color we happily got from Glidden.

An important part of this intercommunication process to understand is that husband and wife don't always agree on what's to be done. Sometimes one sides with the designer or the contractor against the judgment of the other. For example, Tom and I disagreed about the windowpanes, but Tudi agreed with him. He and Tudi felt strongly in favor of windows divided with panes throughout the house. I, on the other hand, was partial to the undivided glass panes in the dining room and kitchen. I liked the fact that the view was uninterrupted.

Another case in point was the art lights. From the very beginning it was important to me that the art have sufficient lighting on the walls, and as we got down to it—closer and closer—Tom designed them, but it wasn't exactly what I wanted. It wasn't that important to him, so it turned out different than I envisioned.

The Daily Visitors

Our new house was only five minutes from our old house and the *Home Improvement* studio, so I was there almost every day. You get caught up in the whole dynamic of the remodeling—building and reshaping. It's as if I could pick up the morning paper with its headline screaming that the end of the world is coming and the first thing I'd turn to was the Orchard Hardware advertisement to see what was on sale.

As Tudi saw it, "I would say Rick was over here a lot. More than I was. Almost every day when he was in town. Pretty much every time he came over, there was a new catch or a new problem. Almost every day."

It was like being pulled by a magnet. Whenever I had some free time, I would find myself over here talking to the workmen:

"Hi, what you guys doing?"

"Oh, putting in this or taking out that."

At times I wondered if the place was ever going to get done, and at the same time worried about how it would look when it did get done.

"Is that going to look okay?"

"Yeah, sure."

"Really? Going to look okay?"

"Yeah, sure."

The other constant presences were the neighbors, or people who claimed to be neighbors—sometimes I wonder if they weren't just burglars casing the place for later, after we moved in. Everybody in that neighborhood walked through our house at some point. It's almost like the construction was an open invitation to browse. The people from whom we bought the house came by to see what we were doing, and the people who owned the house before them came by to see what we were doing, and both of them said pretty much the same thing—that they were intending to put a tile roof on also.

Since the gates were open, people would just walk in and say, "Oh, I always wondered what your house looked like." Of course, since it was torn apart, they still don't know what it looks like from that visit.

Or, people would say, "Hi, we live up the street. We're just over on such-and-such. You know, we love what you're doing with the house!"

Even after we moved in, somebody rang the bell.

"Yeah . . . can I help you?"

"Hi, I walk up and down this street a lot and I always wondered what the backyard looked like."

"Yeah . . . " Then a long, awkward pause.

"Could I see your backyard?"

I didn't know what to say. "Oh, yeah . . . sure, okay."

At least she gave the yard a thumbs-up.

"Oh, wow, big yard." I've never seen her again.

And of course some family, friends, and colleagues from *Home Improvement* would visit as we went along. Tim came by and said it was a warm and friendly place. I remember that Earl Hindman, who plays Tim Allen's half-obscured neighbor on the show, came by and was impressed with the extent of our project. His main observation was that the commercials I was doing on TV must be doing pretty well—he meant that *I* must be doing pretty well because of those commercials I did.

Since I played Al Borland on TV, it affected probably all of the people who worked on the house. As soon as I showed up, they would laugh and kid me. "Oh, this is your house. Well, you should be doing this yourself."

"Oh, couldn't do this yourself, huh?"

And the electricians and the plumbers are like, "I'm thinking of doing this. What do *you* think?"

I think, in some ways, they maybe even worked harder just

to make it nice and right because we had this sense of cama-
raderie among us.

Then there was the time I had a TV news crew coming over
to do a piece on how Al Borland remodels his home, and I
alerted Marty and his people that we would be coming. Of
course, on television I wear my trademarked beard and plaid
shirt. So Marty went to a Hollywood costume shop and got
false beards for everybody and had them come to work wear-
ing plaid shirts so they could all appear on the new program as
Al Borland clones. Unfortunately, Marty chickened out at the
last minute because he thought I might be offended or it might
ruin the story. I would have loved it if he'd gone ahead with it,
and I'm sure the TV people would have as well.

Chaos in the Kitchen

One thing that made us feel good about the total remodeling is that the kitchen looks great—really great. Of course, all we originally planned to do was retile, and instead it became the Olympics of remodeling and probably the most changed room in the house—well, there was the pool table room; and the media room; not to forget the master bedroom; and, also . . . well, we did a lot in the kitchen and it turned out great.

The Cabinets

It started with our trying to decide whether or not to get rid of the cabinets and get new cabinets. Tudi said, "We can get new cabinets."

"Yeah, but how much is that going to be?" I wondered, not that it mattered.

"Yeah, well, you know, it's going to be yada yada yada."

"Ah, well, let's see. The cabinets are fine." You know, now I'm my dad again. The cabinets are fine. "Maybe we'll stain the whole thing."

So we decided we would refinish the cabinets and replace the plain glass doors with antique glass. It sounded simple, but it turned out much more complicated, as did a lot of things we talked about.

So we left the kitchen cabinets in. Later, the cabinets were something I thought we should get rid of, but unfortunately that idea came when we were knee deep in a lot of other things that we were changing, and money seemed pressing.

We had trouble getting colors and stains the way we wanted them in some places, like the pool table room, the dining room, the kitchen, and even on the outdoor lighting fixtures. I began to sympathize with Michelangelo trying to get the colors right on the Sistine Chapel ceiling, and that took seven years!

With the kitchen cabinets, they were lightly stained and we wanted a darker, richer finish. The painter took off a door and painted each side with a different shade of stain for us to choose from. Once we chose, he took all of the cabinet doors to his shop to be beautifully and professionally stained. Unfortunately for us, and ultimately for him, the cabinet doors he brought back were stained much too dark. However, we didn't have the original sample to gauge from since he'd stained that door as well.

Tudi bore the brunt of this problem because I wasn't around at the time. As she explains it, "Well, you were out of town when they were staining the kitchen cabinets. I came in and it looked dark to me, but I thought, 'Oh, it hasn't dried, it'll lighten up.' I said to the cabinet person, 'Oh, that's really pretty.' But in my mind I was saying, 'I don't think the sample was this dark.' So he thought I liked it when I said it's really pretty."

Tudi called me then and said, "It's too dark."

"This is darker than the sample we picked," we said a few days later.

"No, it's the same shade," the cabinet man said.

"Well, show us the sample."

"Well, we stained over the sample."

"So we don't have the original sample?"

"No."

The next day I called Tom and said he had to come see the cabinets because I thought they were too dark, that they were darker than the sample we'd picked out. When Tom came over, we met with the cabinet man.

The cabinet man said, "Well, I thought she liked it. She said it was really pretty."

I answered, "Well, it is really pretty but it isn't the pretty that I wanted here. It's the pretty for somewhere else. It's too dark for here."

Tom agreed that this first stain was too dark. So it came down to, "Who's going to pay to redo this because we don't have the sample door?" It ended up that the cabinet company redid it at their own cost, which was a lot of time and labor.

"Which just shows you, if you have a sample . . . "

"Save it."

"Save it, so you can show them."

You live and learn. We did a whole lot of living and learning in this house.

Tumbled Marble Floor

When we first saw the tumbled marble for the kitchen floor, we said, "We're doing that! Okay!"

And then we got the bid. "What the . . . ?"

It was like seventeen, eighteen grand just for the tile. Expensive, yes, but it looked so great. It had a variety of colors, including beige, brown, and golden tones. The great thing about tumbled marble is that the worn look gives it a feeling of stability. It looks like it's been there forever. So we splurged on the tumbled marble and justified it by telling ourselves we'd save somewhere else. With the tile chosen, the kitchen was on its way to *Better Homes and Gardens*. However, the hardwood flooring that was flowing in from the dining room didn't seem to be on the same level.

I said, "What do we have to do, build a ramp?"

In my mind I was seeing that maybe we could bend the wood flooring so it flowed up to meet the tumbled marble.

Marty, our contractor, shook his head, saying, "This tile [you picked] is pretty thick, so the doorways to the other rooms will have a slope or ridge. We have a three-quarter-inch tile, so the doorways to the other rooms are not on the same level."

"What happened to flush?" I asked. Flush would make me happy.

"Well, it won't work."

I knew he was thinking something, so I said, "What can we do?"

"Okay, the only thing we can do is to pull up the entire kitchen subfloor plywood and lower the floor joists underneath."

Gulp.

"How much will that cost?"

Money pit! It was huge. I don't remember what it was. All I remember is that my mind was racing. Maybe we could make the dining room floor a little high or shave off the tumbled marble so that it flowed, or maybe . . . Oh, man. "What was there before?" I asked.

"Before there was thinner linoleum."

Yeah, they had linoleum that looked like brick.

"Oh, no. That's right. I don't know, why didn't we know this before!? You know, when we were looking at tile, why didn't you say . . . Why didn't somebody . . . Oh, it's nobody's fault! It's clearly nobody's fault, but it's somebody's fault because it's nobody's fault."

Two days later Marty called and said, "I've got an idea . . . We don't have to lower the whole floor, but we can lower the three-quarter-inch plywood that now sits on top of the floor joists. That gives us back the three-quarter inches we need for the tumbled marble to keep it flush."

I could've just kissed Marty. Well, not really. I love it when simple ideas work!

Glass Ceiling Window

When I look at pictures of the kitchen before the remodeling, it doesn't look that much different. They already had the Sub-Zero (refrigerator-freezer) in, the range was different but the center island was there, and, of course, the cabinets were the same only slightly darker. Still, if you look closely, we did some really cool things. We raised the ceiling another foot, the sky-light was there, but we added a divided light window. It was just a plastic bubble skylight before, and now we have something that's more ascetically pleasing. Remember that, originally, Tom wanted to put in safety glass. Safety glass has the wire through it, and my initial reaction was, "I don't want to look up and see my old gymnasium." It reminded me of gym class, and unfortunately, I wasn't very diplomatic about his suggestion. I said, "Oh, that will look terrible!" I tried to explain that I'd like kind of "old" glass—kind of wavy to complement the antique glass in the cabinets.

We knew the antique glass was wavy, but every once in a while we would see water spots in the cabinet glass. On separate occasions, both my wife and I tried to rub off the water spots, only to learn that they weren't water spots, but tiny bubbles in the glass. Shades of Don Ho! We have grown to like it.

When we added the extra height to the ceiling, Tom suggested we put in beams. I think the beams are a really nice addition to the Old World feel of the house. The beams Tom chose for the ceiling were four by six inches, however, when they crossed through the well of the skylight, we thought it would be a wonderful illusion to add another piece to them to make them look as if they were six by six inches. It's a Hollywood prop. Hollywood ceiling beams for a Hollywood house. It's just a little trick that looks good.

Appliances

When it came time to pick a new stove, we found there are a lot to choose from: Wolf makes a great stove; Viking makes a great stove. These are restaurant-quality stoves: free-standing double ovens with burners on top. However, we wanted to go with stacked ovens that stood at a higher and more convenient level, and Tudi wasn't crazy about stainless steel. She felt it was too commercial-like. We got a Viking stove top with stainless steel trim, and white stacked ovens, and microwaves for convenience and no bending—two on each side of the range. The stove has four gas burners along with a griddle and a charbroil grate. We had two microwaves in our previous house and realized that it made things easier, so we carried that over to this house.

When I proposed to Tudi in Zabar's in Manhattan on that luckiest day of my life, her first words were, "You know I hate to cook." Always the optimist, I interpreted that as a yes to my proposal. It turned out she was firm about both things: she would marry me and she didn't like to cook. In our first house, she discovered the joys of having two microwaves and how that made cooking much easier to endure. (No word on whether I am any easier to endure.) So now two microwaves are an integral part of her life and she is never going to be without them. I suspect that if there are no microwaves in heaven, she'll refuse to go.

It occurs to me that I haven't yet talked about how Tudi and I met. So, allow me an indulgence.

In January of 1984, Tudi and I had parts in the Off-Broadway play, *The Other Shore*. We both played characters who didn't appear until the second act, so, as Tudi remembers it: "During the first act, he taught me to play cribbage, which I'd never played before and I've never played since. We played during the first act of every show. It was fun."

After dating for a year and a half, I was thinking, "This is it—this is the one." It was time to ask for her hand in marriage. I decided it would be great to ask her on her birthday. Then I took it a step further and called her mother to find out what time she was born. It was at exactly 12:03 Texas time.

Knowing I was going to do it, but also aware there's no way to direct where someone's going to be at a certain time, I was ready, and when the moment came, we were in kitchenware at Zabar's on the Upper West Side when I popped the question.

Her response was tears and, "You know I hate to cook."

"Yes."

"And, you still want to marry me?"

"Yes."

"Okay, I accept, but why did you ask me in the cooking section of Zabar's?"

"I wanted to ask you to marry me on your birthday at the exact time you were born."

"Was I born at 1:03?"

"No, you were born at 12:03." She just looked at me, and I said, "Texas time!"

The Other Shore was directed by Walter Bobbie, who won a Tony for directing the revival of *Chicago* and is currently directing *Footloose*. But in my opinion his greatest claim to artistic fame is that he cast our marriage. Without him, we might not have met, married, or remodeled.

Ultimately, we knew our future in the theater and in home remodeling was in Los Angeles. The actual decision to move to L.A. came the day Tudi got fed up with our being apart so much and called me at the Players' theater in Columbus, Ohio, where I was appearing in Larry Shue's *The Foreigner*. She announced, "We're moving to Los Angeles." Tudi has always been indecisive like that. So, on my return to New York, we packed our worldly stuff into our beat-up lime-green '74 Buick Apollo, christened it the "Mean Green Driving Machine," and headed west in 1989.

One of the most famous plays in baseball was the double, Tinkers to Evers to Chance. We did it one better with our quadruple strategy based on the cleverness of having friends located a day's drive apart all the way across America. We went from New York to Columbus to Kansas City to Albuquerque to Los Angeles. And, on the fifth day, we rested.

One oddity of our relocating was learning the names of towns important in our lives. I know Seattle was named after Indian chief Seath. Tudi knew San Angelo was named after the founder's wife, Angela de la Garza DeWitt. We both knew New York was named after a city in England. Even so, it took us a long time to discover that the full name of L.A. is "El Pueblo de Nuestra Señora la Reina de los Angeles de Porciuncula." We're not sure what that means, but with all the prickly glitches in our massive remodeling, we think it has something to do with a porcupine.

Of course, there were other things we had to learn about living in California. We knew that when we first drove across the border into the Golden State and were greeted by a sign announcing, "WELCOME TO CALIFORNIA—Financing Available." We knew L.A. was a big town, but we still were surprised when, two miles later, there was another sign, "Los Angeles City Limits—Some Assembly Required."

California is a long, large state that has a crook in the middle, so that Hollywood is farther east than Reno, Nevada. Actually, there isn't just a crook

One-seventh of your life is spent on Monday.

in the middle, there are crooks everywhere, so you have to watch out. The part of California that interested us was Hollywood, which is actually a part of Los Angeles bounded by Mexico, the Pacific Ocean, Santa Barbara, the huge Mojave Desert, and many myths. For example, it is a myth that Santa Barbara is named after Streisand or that the Mojave Desert is actually a set created by Cecil B. DeMille for Charleton Heston in *El Cid*.

The other two things we had to learn, which were easier for Tudi since she's from Texas, where similar situations prevail, had to do with California distances and Spanish names. For example, there are no miles in California. Miles are an archaic form of measurement used by primitives in other parts of North America. Distance in California is only measured in time. You are never fifteen miles from where you're going, you are twenty minutes. As I said, this is easier for Tudi to grasp because in Texas distances are measured by the number of dead armadillos on the road, as in, "Oh, Ralph, lives eight armadillos from here." The other thing that was also easier for Tudi is all the Spanish words common in the basic California vocabulary. For example, Point Mugu is sometimes mistaken as a community for the nearsighted. One of the main rules to understand is that j is pronounced with an h sound, and double l with a y. So "La Jolla" is "La Hoy-Ya." I knew I'd gotten this down when one of our friends asked us how long we'd been in Los Angeles and I answered, "Oh, since Hune or Huly."

The language thing was much the same back when Tudi decided she had to move from Texas to New York if she was going to be a successful actress. One day she decided to make the move and called her parents to tell them. Her mother remembers that call: "Tudi's father said, 'Good. Go ahead.' I just screamed and raved and went to bed."

Of course, Tudi's father used to live and work in New York. He had a feel for the place. He remembers his first business lunch with his boss. "It was a New York lunch, three drinks at the bar and a hot dog from a street vendor on the way back to the office. My boss said, 'You can drink anything you want as long as its not vodka (you can't smell vodka). If you come back to the office and act stupid, I want everybody to know you're drunk and not dumb.'"

So Tudi was off to New York: "I arrived in New York in September and called myself Tudi Texas because I had a pretty strong accent and was oh so green. Of course, I had to make the usual adjustments that newcomers make everywhere, such as the language difference. I remember going out to eat with some new friends. I wanted some soup because it was cold outside. I looked at the menu and asked the waiter, 'What is this mine-stron soup?' I had never heard of minestrone soup before and everybody at the table broke up laughing.

"I admit that I did talk in a Texas dialect at the beginning, so that many New Yorkers couldn't quite understand me. I would use words like 'aig' for what chickens laid and 'bawl' for what water does at 212 degrees, as in, 'Did you bawl those aigs?' 'Arn' is an appliance for smoothing wrinkles, and electrical switches were either 'awn' or 'awf,' as in, 'Is the arn awn or awf?' And all these wonderful variations in speech and customs are what makes uhmurka a great country. One thing that still amazes me is that Texans say 'pa-con' pie, but in New York they say 'pee-can.' That's very hard for me to say. It seems backward to me. Texans should say pee-can."

Anyway, Tudi and I made it to Los Angeles and soon got jobs managing a thirty-unit apartment building in West Hollywood. This meant I spent a lot of time keeping things in repair even though I really didn't know too much about it. Actually, I had the brilliant idea of taking the plumbing apart to see how it worked so I could fix it if anything went wrong. One time I disassembled the shower plumbing without realizing that the shut-off control was hidden behind a shower plate, and all of a sudden water was spraying all over the place. I had to race outside, turn off the main water valve for the whole building, and call the professional maintenance man to fix things. Immediately, there were calls from outraged tenants caught in the middle of showers or laundry, but I explained it was a building emergency. So, I would have an occasional accident, but I got better on my way to becoming Al Borland even before I became Al Borland.

Our coming to L.A. could have been a disaster because, after all, when we arrived we didn't have agents, jobs, or a place to live. If things had gone differently, we might still be catering bar mitzvahs. We called everybody we knew. One friend I called, Andy Cadiff, later said, "It's the move everybody makes. You come out here looking for the pot of gold. I remember the call from Rick. He said, 'I'm out here. I'm gonna give it a go.' Under my breath I said, 'Yeah, you and everybody else.'"

We plowed in doing casting calls, commercial calls, a little theater—everything and anything we could find just as we had done in New York. Soon we were doing soap operas and theater around L.A. We got that job as apartment managers and, in all our spare time, catered at parties, weddings, and bar mitzvahs at the Stephen Wise Temple. Then, to demonstrate my ecumenical talents, I landed a wonderful part playing five dif-

Beverly Hills was originally called "Morocco" and grew out of a bankrupt real estate development involving Will Rogers and the Rodeo Land and Water Company. The first building in the new town was a hotel: the fabled Beverly Hills hotel built in 1912. The second building was Falcon's Lair, a lover's hideaway for Douglas Fairbanks and Mary Pickford, who were then each married to other people. It's surprising the Baptists ever came to town.

ferent roles in *Macbeth*, which was a little tiring because, in most Shakespeare plays, the only one who ever gets to sit down is the king. It was produced by Larry Welch in a theater at the First Baptist Church of Beverly Hills—actually it's more than the First Baptist Church of Beverly Hills. It's the *only* Baptist church in Beverly Hills.

The Kitchen Continued: Surfer-Made Grape Tile

The tile at the back of the stove and on the kitchen counters had that cow motif that was not what we wanted in the kitchen. So we went out in search of new tile. "Going in search of" is something remodelers do more often than Captain Kirk. Going to look at tile was an overwhelming experience because there's a million ways to go, and trying to find what you want is tough. You might find it right away and you might not. We found a tile that we liked that was Old World looking. It was like the glass but it wasn't all smooth. There were some incongruities among the tiles and that gave it the old look we wanted. We found some of the tile at Country Tile, a store Tom likes to work with in Beverly Hills. Then we were referred to a tile factory in downtown L.A., which we discovered supplied that tile to Country Tile. We didn't want to buy the tile directly from the factory because it might have cut out Tom and the Country Tile store of their share, which didn't seem ethical to us. However, we did discover a wonderful decorative trim tile on our own that had a nice grape design to it, and we got that separately for over the stove and on the counter tops. Curiously, this grape tile is made by a surfer in Laguna Beach.

The grape tile became the center of an important point about remodeling as we were preparing for a trip to Italy. I was already nervous about leaving for ten days when I went by the house to casually, closely, inspect the latest developments. By the time I got there, one-quarter of the kitchen had already been tiled. I was looking at the tile that was installed and it didn't dawn on me right away, but something looked odd. As I looked longer, it slowly came to me that the wonderful grape leaf tile was being installed with the grapes hanging up. Now this may have something to do with their getting enough sun to mature, or not installing a wine grape tile before its time, but it looked odd to me.

I said, "You know, I think grapes grow down."

The tile man said, "Well, it's a design and it could go either way." He'd already done half of that wall so he probably liked the idea of grapes that defied gravity.

"I would really like it to hang down."

He said, "Well, over the stove it's in a square so it will have to go up."

"Okay, that little piece will go up and everything else will go *down*."

You know, you're leaving the creation of your baby in somebody else's hands to make something permanently wrong. It makes you a little uneasy.

Of course, as soon as you put anything in the house, you will find ten things that are just as cool. You will look for *months* for what you want or what you see in your mind, and you'll ultimately find it and put it in. Miraculously, the next day you'll see ten other things that are just as cool. That's just the way it works.

Wine and Spice and Everything Not So Nice

I wanted a wine rack at the end of the kitchen island. What I envisioned was a triangular arrangement of wine bottle slots made of solid wood going from the front of the rack to the back of the rack with no open spaces around each slot. This would allow each bottle to lie completely supported on its side the full depth of the rack. Instead, the workman built an open, crisscross work rack so the horizontal bottles were supported only at the front and rear of the rack. Which wasn't what I wanted. That taught me you have to be very specific when you explain something to the people doing the work. You can't just say, "I want a wine rack in here." You have to say, "I want a wine rack and I want it to look like this. . . ." Tom had the same idea I did, but the workman didn't have the picture in his head that either Tom or I had.

This is another key point about remodeling—namely, there are misunderstandings throughout the whole process. Sometimes the contractor doesn't understand what you want; sometimes the workman doesn't understand what the contractor wants; and sometimes nobody seems to understand what anybody wants. It is just different minds seeing the same thing different ways.

A case in point was the great Knob Countdown. This involved Tudi, Tom, and Tom's assistant, Jan, who all stood in the kitchen to count how many knobs, pulls, and handles were needed before they went out to shop for the kind we wanted. The knobs go on cabinet doors, pulls go on drawers, and handles are on the larger doors.

So all three of them counted separately, and one said, "I got thirty-two."

Another said, "No, no. I got thirty-one."

"Okay, let's count again."

Once more they could not agree on the count. They literally spent forty minutes counting, recounting, and rerecounting until they finally agreed on a number. Then they ordered them and it was still wrong!

Then we had the cabinet handle caper where handles were put on both sides of some cabinet doors, which looked symmetrically fine except the handles on the hinge side obviously could not open the door—they were just decorative. I actually kind of liked it, but neither Tudi or Tom did. It appealed to my sense of humor.

The spice rack is still another case in point. It was created in a drawer by the stove, with the idea of holding spice containers lying at an angle so the labels could be read. Apparently, no one thought to use actual spice containers to check the sizes, and the drawer was built with holders too close together. If you actually put spice containers in the drawers, you couldn't close the drawers.

This also raises another important point about design and construction, namely, the people who do the designing and constructing often don't have to use what they've created.

Rick's Kitchen Tips

The kitchen is one of the busiest and most important rooms in the house. Here are some tips we've learned about making it pleasant, safe and efficient.

- *The Door-Drawer Clash.* Most storage space in your kitchen (refrigerator-freezer, cabinets, closets, and drawers) opens into the kitchen space. Before you build them or install them, measure carefully. Make sure there's enough room for the doors to swing open and the drawers to pull out freely.

- *Left-Right Door Option.* These days most refrigerator-freezers are made with doors that either hinge on the right or the left. Check to see which is the best for your kitchen.

- *The Forgotten Inside Space.* Besides the door-drawer clash, check your plans to be sure the space *inside* the cabinets, closets, and drawers are the right size and dimensions for what you plan to put inside them. For example, make sure the closet is tall enough to hold the mops and brooms you want to store there. Same with drawers and cabinets. Sound silly? Take the case of our too-small spice drawers in our carefully planned and expensive kitchen.

- *Kitchen Triangle.* The heart of the kitchen is the triangle that is frequently formed by the sink, the stove, and the refrigerator. Try not to have ordinary foot traffic walking through this area and disrupting things.

- *Appliance Trap.* Today, there seems to be an appliance for everything, from making bread to brewing beer. Even if you could afford all these expensive gadgets, you haven't got room for them all. So, right at the start, make a priority list. Decide what you absolutely must have, what you can afford, and what you have room for in the kitchen. Obviously, you need an appliance to make things hot: a stove and oven. Also, you need an appliance to keep things cold: a refrigerator-freezer.

Those are the basics. From there on, add only what you need and have the budget and space to get.

Niagara Falls, Toilet Tissue, and Other Charmin Tales

One day I was standing in my son's room and I called to Tudi. We heard the sound of rushing water coming from under the floor.

I'm thinking, "What is that?" and called the contractor, Marty, in to listen with us.

He said, "What? I don't hear anything."

That was a joke, of course, so I asked again, "Marty, are we going to hear this?"

"Oh, no, once you put the carpeting in and everything and then, of course, we'll wrap the pipe. That'll get it."

So they did all that and it was still very loud. He called the plumber to come back and fix it. He had run the water line from the street under the house to the backyard, where it served the pool and the sprinklers. The sprinklers were on a timer set to come on in the middle of the night, which would make all that noise even more disrupting. It was loud—Niagara Falls loud.

"Can't we quiet this down?" I asked the plumber.

He changed the pressure and wrapped the pipes in more insulation, but nothing worked. I suppose we could have pretended to live in Venice, where the sound of water under the floorboards is romantic.

In such situations it's helpful to understand the native sounds of the great plumbing hunter on safari. When he makes the noise, "Hmm-mm," that means he doesn't know what's wrong and is going to spend more time—with the meter running—coming up with his guess. The sound "ugh" means he's found the trouble and it's going to make a mess of your bathroom, besides costing more than you figured and less than he hoped. Small children should be immediately sent from the room when you hear, "Uh-oh!" This means it's still going to cost more than you figured but as much or more than he hoped, and he'll make a mess. Anglo-Saxon expletives normally follow "Uh-oh," either from him or from you. Usually, from you. And finally there's "Darn!" This means he's found the trouble, it will be expensive and messy, but he left a critical tool or critical part "back at the shop."

Finally, concerning our little problem, after going through all of the above we all agreed that rerouting the water system was the thing to do. This plumbing change was on Marty's ticket, illustrating that the best time to catch mistakes is right away. If you call the contractor's attention to errors while workmen are still on the job, the problems can be corrected then and there—often with no extra cost. If you don't bring it up until weeks later, when the contractor and workmen have moved on to another job, it will probably cost you extra for them to come back. That's why the final walk through the house with the contractor is very important—so you can catch what still needs to be done before everybody moves on to another project.

A mathematical curiosity hovered above these changes: as I added, they multiplied in number while subtracting from my bank account.

Then there was the day the plumber came out from under the house and said, "In twenty-five years in this business, I have never seen anything like it." I felt another Change Order coming on. Part of the gas line system, we discovered, was made of thin quarter-inch aluminum pipe instead of galvanized steel pipe. The odd part was that aluminum pipe had only been

Historic Building Blunders
The Great Pentagon Piping Mistake

We were not the only ones with plumbing problems. The Pentagon, noted for enormously expensive hammers and toilet seats, is also in the building blunder game with everyone else. In one case, it built a huge building for testing Air Force jet engines. This required a maze of complicated tubing and piping throughout the very expensive structure. For some reason, stupidity probably, the people designing the tubing never met or talked with the people designing the piping, and it apparently never occurred to the people in charge of those people that they should meet and talk with each other. You, of course, have already figured out the result: the complex tubing didn't fit the complex piping and neither fit into the building built to house them. So the building had to be rebuilt for an extra $138 million.

used on part of the gas line—not all of it. In any case, the aluminum was soft and easy to cut. Actually, a pair of flimsy plastic cutters could cut it. This network of gas pipes had to be replaced with steel piping. I wondered why the man I paid to inspect the house before they closed escrow didn't discover

> You have to accept that some days you're the pigeon and some days you're the statue.
> — my father, Gene

this discrepancy. I never got an answer but it may have escaped his notice because the aluminum pipe had been painted black and that made it look more substantial.

They call it being "escrowed," but more and more I think they are pronouncing it wrong.

This brings up another important point for all remodelers to remember. Keep a record of names and numbers of everybody who works on your house and, particularly, of inspectors. If the inspection was shoddy and something is wrong later, you know who to go back to for an explanation.

I know part of the problem was people not communicating with each other. And, of course, as the remodeling went along, we would order changes as we saw new possibilities, including the possibility of owing more than the entire French national debt. Even so, it was often a breakdown in communications between Tudi and me or the two of us and the contractor.

Throughout the remodeling process I would come in, stand, and try to envision how it would turn out. For example, one day I was in the master bathroom and saw a comfortable-sized shower where, a few days later, I found a gigantic built-in wooden bench taking up half the space. When I asked the contractor where it came from, he showed me a dotted line on the approved blueprints—a wooden bench, soon to be tiled. I said we weren't going to take a nap while taking a shower. The bench was removed. That was another Change Order, for about $500 because it had already been waterproofed and sealed into place.

Then, amazingly, everybody forgot about toilet paper. It

turned out that when the four bathrooms were finished, there were no practical places to mount the toilet paper holders. Maybe if you're building a house from scratch, you can do better, but we had to work with what we had. In two of those bathrooms, we changed the toilet area, and in changing it, did not consider where the toilet paper holder was going to go.

That was really a designer's goof.

Still, Tudi did like many of the things Tom did for us: "He was very good creatively and aesthetically. The two-story entry was his idea and it makes a huge difference. It's beautiful. He has wonderful ideas and he does beautiful work."

The Remodeling Adventure in Other Rooms

Entry Hall and Powder Room

Just off the front entry hall is the guest powder room where we relocated the toilet, installed a new commode, and replaced what had been a vanity table sink with a standing pedestal sink that we liked better. These fixtures came from the Kohler company people whom I had the pleasure of meeting at the AT&T golf tournament in Pebble Beach, which happened to coincide with the fact that I needed lots and lots of bathroom fixtures. Was my old friend Serendipity playing in that same golf tournament? A few months later they invited me to tour their family-owned company in Kohler, Wisconsin, near Sheboygan. I saw how the commodes and sinks are enameled in the firing process—all very interesting, and then we visited the museum of all their products made over the years. It's amazing what a few pictures and handshakes will do. They gave me a good deal on sinks, tubs, and faucets for the house. We used Kohler throughout the house, except for that one pedestal sink that Tom got for the guest powder room in a design Kohler didn't make.

The Kohler experience reminds me that, when I think of how expensive some of the remodeling seemed, it was not nearly as expensive as it might have been. For example, there's a designer, Sherle Wagner, who is famous for her twenty-four-karat, gold-plated washbasins and swan faucets. She also has created a commode carved out of rose aurora marble with a rose quartz control lever and gold-leaf seat cover. This is available for only $10,666, and the great news is that there's also a matching bidet that can be had for $9,823, and washbasin for only $8,400.

It was in this guest powder room that we first used what looks like wallpaper but is actually painted plaster walls. The design is hand-painted and stenciled by Esther, a very talented painter from Kentucky, whom Tom uses a lot. It is a style called "faux" painting or "faux finis," which is French for false finish. By using various paints, glazes, stencils, and application techniques involving sponges, rags, plastic wrap, and brushes, the artist can create the look of all sorts of material such as wood, marble, stone, and so on to suit the taste of the artist or home owner. For example, in our living room fireplace, the hearth must be real marble and fireproof to meet the fire safety code. The mantel over the fireplace, however, is wood, and to blend that with the marble hearth we had Esther put a faux finis on that imitates the marble. The simplest faux finishes are done in two or more colors or shades of the same color. Faux has become very popular in home decoration to create a warm feel of mature surfaces. Remember that one of the things we liked about Tom's work was that it didn't look as if it were brand-new or "designed," but rather, that it had always been that way. The faux finish technique used by Esther helped give that feeling.

As a result, we had her work throughout much of the house on most of our walls. Of course, if we ever have to repaint them, it would be hard to do ourselves because it's not just a color on the walls, it's a mesh of several colors.

Originally, the front door entryway near the guest powder room had a nine-foot ceiling, with a coat closet jutted out into what was already a cramped space. This is where we employed one of the first remodeling ideas that Tom came up with. We cut back the coat closet and raised the ceiling up to about thirty feet. What was a narrow lower entry hall was transformed into something much more welcoming. We put in a wrought-iron chandelier with lighted sconces and windows up high to illuminate the ceiling and give it a sense of space. Then I had the idea to put up niches for artwork in spots throughout the house. However, you want to come up with ideas like this before the walls are built and plastered so you can run wiring for lighting. That's why the niche in the entry has no light.

The wrought-iron chandelier in the entry hall was still another example of missed communication among the three of us. Tudi and Tom did another of those "go out to find" trips that took them to the Los Angeles Design Center, where scores of decorators and manufacturers have display showrooms open to designers and to the public. I think every metropolitan area probably has one by this time. Tudi saw a lovely wrought-iron chandelier in one of the showrooms that she told me about when she came home. She said I should go see it to decide if I liked it for the front entry hall. Well, I went over there a few days later and I hated it. So that was the end of that—almost. Only later did we find out that they had changed the chandelier on display between the time Tudi and Tom were there and when I came by. When we got that sorted out and I saw the chandelier Tudi had seen, I liked it immediately, and that's the one we installed.

As the time moved along and things were getting done, they were starting to put up metal brackets for the drywall panels to give them a nice straight edge. It took me a few days to realize that I actually wanted the inside walls plastered with what are called bull-nosed edges, instead of the painted drywall that they were getting ready to install. Whether I was in denial or not, I just assumed that we would plaster. Of course, I forgot that old saying: "When you assume, you make an ass of u and me."

Tudi and I discussed this, and we came to the conclusion that plaster-covered walls were what we wanted.

"Because our other house had regular wallboard that was painted."

"Drywall, painted . . . But it was a whole different kind of house."

"And, originally, this house had drywall that was painted."

"Yeah, and originally we were doing only the master bedroom and the kitchen."

So as they started tacking up the metal for the straight edge on the walls, it dawned on me that I wasn't going to get the bull-nosed edges that I envisioned. That's when I talked to Tom and Marty, with Change Order #43 being the result. So that item went from $4,320 in the original bid to $13,923. Again, the original bid was not sufficient for my visualization.

Dining Room

Directly off the entry hall and between the kitchen and the pool table room is the dining room, where we raised the ceiling as much as we could and where we learned another remodeling lesson.

Tudi recalls, "We had a meeting with Tom to pick out paint colors for the baseboard in the dining room and he was delayed. So by the time we met, it was getting dark. We got one of the big work lights with the grill over it into the dining room and began looking at paint samples on pieces of wood that had the stria." (A design pattern of very thin, parallel lines of color.) "We chose the color for the baseboards, molding, and other trim."

Much later, when the work was done, it was the kitchen stain strain and déjà vu all over again. I said, "That isn't what we picked because what we chose was kind of blue—it has a blue in it."

And Tom said, "No, no. This is the one."

This time the sample was saved. He brought back the sample pieces for us to see, and sure enough, it was the one we picked, but we'd selected it in the artificial light. I thought it had more blue in it, but obviously I was wrong. I came to like this color, but thought I'd picked a whole different hue.

Rick's tip for picking colors: It's best to look at your color samples at night with artificial light *and* during the day with natural light.

"If you really looked closely at the stenciling in the ceiling, it has a little more blue in it than the trim does. You can't really tell because they are too far apart, but that's what I thought I was matching and ended up not. Another lesson."

The Pool Table Room

Originally, the pool table room had a linoleum flooring on top of concrete slab, and a lower ceiling, all painted white, with free-standing bookshelves on one side. On the far end was the leaded glass window looking into the dining room, and a wet bar standing in front of that. There was one door with windows on either side of it leading to the backyard.

My vision for this room was something that was much warmer and incorporated a lot of things that I wanted to tuck away into one room. First, I knew that this was going to be a pool table room. I knew I wanted to have a place for books, a library. I knew I wanted it in wood. I wanted the ceilings and the walls paneled, with an area for books, and then, I don't know whose idea the aquarium was, but since we were throwing everything else into this room, an aquarium seemed like a good idea too. At some point I thought about leaving the leaded glass window there, having a waterfall window where water can come down on either side of the glass. That was not something Tom liked. He felt that, with all the paneling and shelves, the waterfall window would have made the room a little more lopsided, but I kept the idea of the waterfall window in my mind for about half a year, until we started looking at the plans for the pool table room.

As an example of how Tom and I worked together, I told Tom that I pictured the pool table room in mahogany. He said, "Okay, we can do this in mahogany, and I want to put slat backs"— looks somewhat like tongue and groove—"on all the shelves."

"Slat backs?" I said.

"Yeah, to make it look more Old World."

At the time, all I could think of was these old cabinets that we used to have up at the lake house in Seattle that had been painted over, over and over again, and I went, "That doesn't seem too cool. I don't like that idea." So I talked him out of that, saying, "No, no, I want a nice solid back. We'll keep it in mahogany. There will be other details to look at, but I don't want that."

It was interesting, and here's another bit of remodeling wisdom: once he mentioned the slats idea to me, I began to see it in a lot of stores and other places and I got more comfortable with the idea. Then, by the time we were going to have the kitchen cabinets stained, he said, "Well, do you mind if I put these slats in the kitchen cabinets?"

I go, "Yeah! Yeah! I think that'll look great."

Further, we used the slatted back for the hutch in the breakfast area, and when he designed the cabinets for the media room, I thought the slatted look on the back of the cabinets looked great there, too. I think my original reservation about the slatted look came from watching my dad build things. He liked everything smooth, which is a little bit more modern as opposed to the slatted look, which is a little bit more rustic. So

> Genius has its limits. Stupidity knows no bounds.

I had that bit of carryover taste from my dad on some things.

The room has one design feature that I brought in from *Tool Time* that is, literally, very cool. We installed refrigerated drawers for wine and drinks under the TV set. This idea came from an episode on the show about space saving. There's a company that makes refrigerator drawers for kitchens that aren't big enough for a full-size refrigerator. These work well for extra vegetable storage next to your sink or cutting board area. I decided to use them in the pool table room for beer and wine. I saw these again at a trade show where I learned all the particulars from the people who make them, the folks at Sub-Zero.

Tom and I worked pretty closely on the shelving in this room. All the walls are made for books, but underneath the shelves are enclosed cabinets. It had always been my intention that the room have a paneled look, with the ceiling being paneled, parts of the walls that aren't shelves being paneled, and then the base, beneath the shelves, looking like panels, even though they were cabinets. So instead of having knobs, we went with push-pull latches. The cabinet designer came up with the idea of running a wooden bead to overlap the door joints so you can't tell they're cabinets. I also wanted to be able to take the shelves out but didn't want little holes and holders. So they created a special wire bracket for holding up shelves that didn't leave big holes. I wanted the shelf dividers to be a little more substantial and wider than what was normal, so instead of the one-inch wide standard dividers, we used three-inch dividers.

You may not think it would be possible to put more stuff into this room, but you underestimate us. I did get the large aquarium. That's worked out well. I've built it into the wall against a small service room under the stairway to the second floor. This service room has an outside entrance that makes it easy to service the tank. Whose idea it was depends on whom you speak with, myself or my wife. In the year and a half since we put it in, we now don't know who came up with the original idea, but a large aquarium is something I always wanted, and it seemed this room was the only practical place to put it. Guys on the whole tend to be a little more inarticulate about certain things, whereas women, more times than not, will vocalize. The idea might come to both of you at the same time, but whoever gets it out of their mouth first gets to claim the credit. So I think this was my idea, but I'm not sure. Sometimes I have an idea in my head, but it's Tudi who vocalizes it. That's part of the mystic communication of marriage, when I think and Tudi talks.

The lights in the pool table room were another compromise between what I wanted and what Tom and Tudi wanted. Tudi said: "Originally, Rick wanted recessed lighting in the ceiling, but Tom and I both talked him out of it because it wasn't Spanish Mediterranean—it's more deco. I understood wanting it because it adds such a great atmosphere to a room, but I felt it didn't really mesh with the style of the house That's one of the few times Rick and I weren't connecting in our vision."

I said, "By the way, we were just in Italy and there seemed to be a lot of recessed lighting."

"Yes there was, but it was in modern, contemporary, Italy. It wasn't old Italy, which is more like what we were doing. The recessed light cans in the ceiling are small and they're all on dimmers so it doesn't look like a screaming overhead light."

At the end of the pool table room is the staircase to the second floor. Tom suggested we go with a wrought-iron railing with a mahogany handrail. Immediately my mind went to the wrought-iron railings that I grew up with outside the house in Seattle. It was simple and plain and most of the houses on the block had it and it didn't seem that extraordinary. Considering that we were going to put this kind of railing into this elegant mahogany room, the idea of wrought iron—like the slat-back shelves—was one I couldn't go with. So Tom talked me into looking at a similar railing that he'd installed in the home of a friend of his. As we were going to this friend's house, Tom mentioned that it was the home of Stephen Topolowsky. I looked at him, thinking he was kidding.

I asked, "Stephen Topolowsky, the actor?"

Tom goes, "Yes, do you know him?"

"Do I know him? I owe him this house. If it was not for Stephen, we wouldn't be driving over to his house to look at wrought-iron railings! He would have taken the role of Glenn on *Home Improvement* and I would have ended up being an apartment house manager in West Hollywood."

As luck would have it, Stephen was not there, because in my state I would not have been able to face him with the knowledge of having not only taken his job but used his designer as well. I immediately saw that Tom was right. This type of mahogany and wrought-iron handrail was perfect for what we wanted.

However, when the wrought-iron craftsman installed the railing, there was something about the lintel post wrought iron that wasn't right. The wrought iron was too short, and instead of going down to the step, it stopped too soon. Here again we would learn another remodeling lesson, because we spent a week and a half agonizing over it and, finally mentioned it to Tom, who mentioned it to the craftsman. The craftsman's reaction was, "Oh, no problem. I can fix that." Moreover, he did.

Living Room

In the living room, Esther did her magic faux painting again, just as she did throughout the house on some walls and ceilings and the living room fireplace mantel. With the ceiling beams in the living room, the painters striated them and brushed on color with a dry paintbrush to simulate wood texture. After that they sanded it down to make it look weathered or antiqued. Just as with the faux beams in the kitchen, the living room beams were not really structural, only decorative. In a sense, that's in keeping with the imagery that made Hollywood famous.

The cosmetics used throughout the house have the reverse purpose of cosmetics used by women. The house cosmetics are designed to make it look glamorous by appearing older than it is, while women's cosmetics are designed to make them look glamorous by appearing younger than they are. There is some deep, meaningful message here, but it escapes me. Perhaps it's only faux philosophy.

Getting
There

Playroom

As you leave the living room heading for the master bedroom, you encounter a small guest bedroom we decided to covert into a combination guest bedroom and playroom for Cooper. As usual, we had endless meetings about the details. Roosevelt, Churchill, and Stalin had fewer meetings at Yalta, and they were dividing up the continent of Europe. We were just trying to settle on the color of the tile in the bathroom of Cooper's playroom.

We all talked about retiling the shower. Tom also wanted to relocate the sink, which had a window over it. Tom wanted to move it and have a mirror over it instead. He said, "I happen to hate that. I like mirrors over the sink when you're washing your face, shaving, whatever. . . ."

Tudi said, "I agree."

"So, what we can do is move the sink over to another wall with a mirror and leave the window where it is."

"Okay, go away and send us a bid on this."

For changing the sink around and retiling this bathroom, it was ludicrous . . . it was like $20,000 or something. We were just going to move a sink, after all, not raise the *Titanic*. Originally, I didn't want to change anything in this bathroom. This was the playroom bathroom, after all. No one was going to see it, so who cares? It was yellow with yellow tile and . . .

Tudi said, "Hated it."

At that point I was thinking, this is where we can save some money. Let's just not do this bathroom. But it was important to Tudi that this bathroom be changed. She hated the yellow tile. . . .

"Hated it."

"It was yellow linoleum on the floor and yellow tile on the sink," Tudi recalls. "It had a really dirty white shower with grouting that was originally white but had turned black. It was awful and there was no cleaning it . . . it was a redoing thing, not a cleaning thing. I don't remember what the bid was except it was ridiculous. So I said, 'Keep the sink where it is with the original wood and everything. Retile the countertop and put in a new sink'—the old one was cracked. 'Retile the shower too.' Then, somewhere in there, I came to a meeting and realized Rick had talked to Tom and they also decided to change the shower door because the existing one was so ratty and old. In addition, we were going to replace the toilet because it had a crack in the tank.

"So we went to the appliance store, ordered the dishwasher and looked at toilets. We said, 'Well, this type in the master bathroom, this style in the powder room, and this style will go in Cooper's bathroom, and this style in Cooper's playroom.' So we picked out five toilets to order from Kohler and thought that's the end of it— to coin a phrase.

"Meanwhile, we hadn't changed the shower door in the playroom yet. In this bathroom the toilet is right by the shower and hinged on the right so you can hardly open the door past the toilet. When we sat on this toilet before, we didn't even think about that. We didn't measure the toilet, but fortunately Rick realized that if we got the size toilet we had in mind, the shower door wouldn't open. We said, 'Okay, we need a smaller toilet so the shower door will open.' Then Rick said, 'I hate teeny toilets. You're trying to go to the bathroom and it's teeny. I hate it.' Well, you're not even going to use this toilet . . . ever.

"Finally, we said, 'Okay, we'll get a medium size instead of the small size because the large size wouldn't fit.' Then someone said, 'Just get a different shower door—one that opens from the other side.' Well, duh! It was a simple solution that wasn't obvious at the beginning. So, we did that.

"Over this stupid little bathroom, we had way too many

meetings, 'Change thats,' and 'Send us thoses,' We had all these meetings and, in my opinion, a lot was my fault because, as Rick said, I hated the yellow. We were doing so well with the rest of the house, why leave that one room looking unfinished?"

During all this, I recall telling Tudi, "With the rest of the house looking great, this room can be an example of what it used to look like."

"No," she told me. "We can take pictures and show them pictures of what it used to look like."

Then I had another idea—we should get a montage of the old bathroom and put it in the new bathroom. "It's a great idea!" I said. "Get pictures of the old rooms and put them up in the new rooms."

Tudi voiced a different view: "I don't think that's such a great idea."

Son Cooper's Room

"We were going to put the whirlpool bathtub from the master bathroom into Cooper's room, but it didn't fit," Tudi explained. "So we gave it to friends. We also gave away the kitchen sink. We got a brand-new sink for the kitchen, but it was not the one I wanted. So they ordered another one, and the first new one just sat in the garage. Some of our friends had just bought a house and said, "We're going to redo our kitchen."

"Do you need a kitchen sink?" we asked. "We have one."

So they took it home. This was Nancy, Tudi's childhood friend from "S'nangelo," Texas, and her husband, Todd Allen. The next time they came over, they brought a croquet set because we had room for croquet and a whole edition of books for our library because they didn't have room for that either. So we traded: a sink for croquet and books.

Master Bedroom

We started on the remodel of the master bedroom without thinking we would remodel the master bathroom. It had brand-new tiles, brand new sinks, tub, commode—everything was brand-new except for the shower. The shower was 1940s.

We opened up the entryway to the bedroom and had plans to add a fireplace. This fireplace was not actually built until we were almost halfway through the whole house remodeling. So we were in and out of that master bedroom for months and they were remodeling everything else and, then, one day we walked in and there was this huge box there. That's what caught our attention because they built it with a mammoth hearth and we walked in and said, "Uh, we're not doing plays in here." It was like a stage, and we had to have them cut it down to less than half the size from what it was originally.

Beyond that, we were pushing out one wall to make the bedroom bigger, and when we dug down to prepare the foundation for the master bedroom extenuation, we found foundations from a previous civilization. We're not sure how old this ancient foundation was except there was a stone tablet marked Change Order LXVII signed by somebody named Marc Anthony. It had instructions that the pyramid veranda should be done by Tuesday when the Pharaoh comes.

Tudi remembers the carpeting problems in particular: "In our many, many carpet hells—I will always call it that—I think the one in the master bedroom was definitely the first. We knew what we wanted, we ordered it, it came in and they installed it. That was great and it seemed so simple, but I should have known better. After it was installed, I found something I didn't expect: a huge seam. Of course, you have to have a seam because this room is so big. So, there's a seam, but it sticks up noticeably . . . it really sticks up.

Historical Building Blunders
The "Other" Pyramid

Everybody thinks the pyramids at Giza we see today are marvels of construction, but not all the ancient pyramids survived. The pyramid at Meidum has disintegrated because of a human design flaw. The foundation was put on sand rather than rock, as with other pyramids, and the foundation blocks are horizontal instead of tilted inward. These relatively small design variations meant that earthquakes that did not affect other pyramids made the foundation of the Meidum Pyramid shift and brought down the walls it was holding up.

"So, I called Tom and I said, 'You need to get back over here because I don't want this seam showing the way it does.'

"In our conversation, Tom said this was a low-pile carpet, but I said that I couldn't imagine the seam had to show that much and it was the only seam in the room. Tom came over, got on his knees and looked at the seam. He says, 'Yeah, they sewed two of the rows together instead of one.' It also was rising up. I don't know why they did that. He called the carpet people and they came out and said it had to be that way for it to hold together. They couldn't do anything about it. So Tom calls in his other carpet people, who didn't lay this carpet. They came and looked at it and said, 'Well, you know, I don't think it has to be the two rows, but we can't take it out now, because it

> Lord, grant me the serenity to accept the things I can not change, the courage to change the things I can, and the wisdom to hide my mistakes under another coat of paint.

will show.' So we have a big seam running down the middle of the room.

"The sound speakers mounted in the master bedroom wall remind me that, when they were installed, the mesh covering the speaker was white. When they were put in on the fauxed wall, they were really noticeable, and we asked them to paint those as well.

"They painted them and, because the mesh holes were so small, the paint sealed them up. They had to reopen the mesh by hand. We came over one day and the painters are outside poking little holes in it with toothpicks. Talk about high-tech remodeling."

Rick's tip: By the way, these are the same toothpicks that I use on my Hillshire Lil' Smokies.

When we bought the house, there was no door in the master bedroom going directly into the bedroom closet. You had to go into the bathroom and through a door from there into the walk-in closet. There was also an outside window at the end of the closet. Why would you have a window in your clothes closet? Maybe they wanted to check the outside weather to see what they should wear, or perhaps model what they were going to wear for passersby to get their reaction. Whatever the reason, we sealed up the window and put up a new full-length mirror in its place.

We originally said to Tom, "When we do this master bedroom, we want our existing furniture to work in here because we like our furniture and it was an investment."

He said, "Oh, yes, absolutely."

So, as they're building it we would stand in the middle and say, "Where can we put the long dresser? Where can we put the short dresser?" We had a long dresser, a short dresser, and an armoire, and it ended up that the only piece that fit when they were done building was the long dresser.

We had the benefit of being able to dictate what we wanted done in that room, and then nothing fit after we said what we wanted. We thought of putting the short dresser into the walk-in closet and the armoire at the foot of the bed. But then we redesigned the closet and there was no room for the dresser. After we put in the fireplace, there was no room for the armoire.

"So that's when we shifted the armoire and built a wall around it." Tudi continues, "Now, it will have to stay here if we ever move, which we never will in our life."

Here again came the tumbling dominoes. Once we got the armoire in there, we realized that it seemed stubby or puny and we added another case above it so the perspective looked right. Then that shifted the look of the room and Tom decided that an arch entrance to the bedroom was needed to give it a finished look. That, in turn, required relocating one of the air intake openings of the heating/cooling system. Who would've thought it?

On the plus side, Tom came up with a great feature in the master bathroom. We each have our own areas in the bathroom. In the wall behind one drawer of each of our units, Tom put an electric outlet into which each of our hair dryers is plugged. So you open the drawer and take out the hair dryer and it's already plugged in, ready to use. When you're finished, you simply replace the dryer in the drawer and slide it closed— no plugging or unplugging. I thought that was so excellent. That's why we have designers, because they know that stuff.

Media Room

This is a room that wasn't part of the original house design. It's just a room that was added on to the end of what was a long house anyhow—I think it's a toll call to phone the master bedroom from the media room. This room was obviously a new addition because all the windows were metal, unlike any of the other windows in the house. Also, for whatever reason that is now lost to the world, the previous owners decided to drop it below sea level. So when you enter the room, you step down even though there really was no structural need for this and it would have benefited from staying on the same level with the rest of the house. It was just a 1960s-style sunken room. Even so, we decided not to raise the floor to make it level with the rest of the house because we would have also had to raise the roof. However, the walls were soundproofed with a beige padding. Now it's a great soundproof room for big-screen TV, and you can turn up *Terminator* full blast and no one is going to hear it.

Another feature in the media room reminds me we sometimes plan too far ahead. We first thought we would put a cabinet against another wall in this room. At the time, the wall was still open and had an air vent for the heating system which came out near the floor. If we put a cabinet against the wall, it would block that vent, so I had them shift the vent to the top of the wall. When we changed our minds and didn't put a cabinet there, it left the vent marooned high on the wall and more visible than we would prefer. So much for planning ahead!

For this room, I asked Tom to design me a wall unit and a corner desk. The last desk I'd had built for me was done by my father when I was a kid in school and wanted to buy a desk. Instead, my dad said, "Since we have a table saw in the basement, why don't I just build you one?"

"Oh, man," I said. "No, you don't have to build me a desk."
Looking back now, I realize I was wrong, he *did* have to build
me a desk. He built this huge, beautiful desk with a wood
Formica top. It wasn't what I envisioned having, but he built it
and it was special. It was a great desk. It killed him to go out
and buy things that he thought he could just build in the basement. When he built a house, my dad built the cabinets himself,
and when he'd replace old cabinets, he would take them out
and store them in the garage for another time. That's probably
why I have trouble throwing anything away. The desk is still in
my room at home, and Dad's still using my desk.

This time, I was ordering a new cabinet and desk for
myself, but when we got the plans and they bid on it, they were
a little more expensive than I'd anticipated. Well, actually a *lot*
more expensive than I anticipated. So I took the plans and
went somewhere else to see what it would cost to have them
build it, and they came in at just about half the price. I gave
them the plans and said, "Okay, build this for me." I'd already
paid for the plans, so I figured I might as well use them. The
guy came out and took the measurements just to make sure,
and apparently his measurements were wrong. When the unit
finally got here, the cabinet didn't quite fit.

They also failed to take into account a vertical wall beam,
so the unit doesn't fit flush against the wall. Even so, it's a
beautiful unit and it really finishes off this room. We wanted it
to be a little more rustic-looking, so the unit is distressed
knotty pine with the tongue-and-groove effect at the back.
Looking back, I see were we needlessly spent money to get fur-
nishings with that "distressed look." With a six-year-old boy in
the house, we have our own little distresser. I remember I
made a big deal about "distressing" a coffee table we got, but
Cooper, from day one, climbs on it, bangs on it, and has given it
a more distinct aged look.

If Only We Had Sinbad to Help with the Carpets

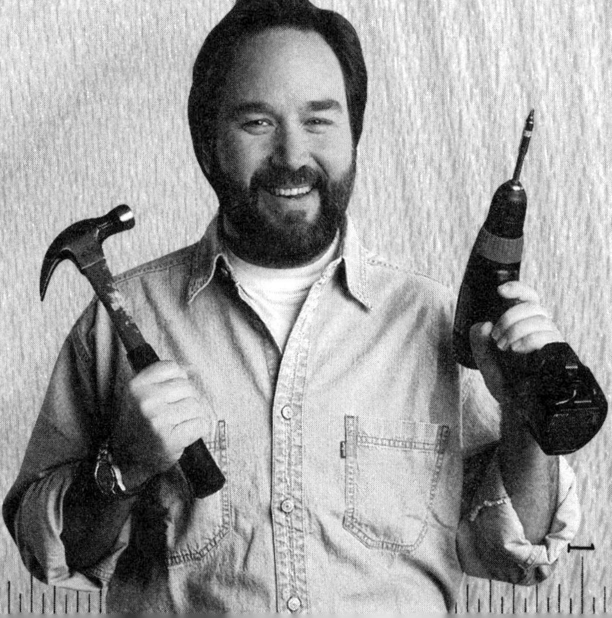

The carpets were good and bad news rolled up in one. The good news was that picking carpet meant we were close to the end. The carpeting was the last major item to go in the house. The bad news was the hunt for the right color and texture.

After looking and looking, Tudi exclaimed in frustration, "This is not the Holy Grail we're looking for here!" She was right. The Holy Grail would have been easier to find.

When the day came to pick the carpeting, I couldn't be there. I told Tudi, "You know I like the one that our friend Shelly has."

So the designer came over with fifty carpet samples that he and his assistant carried into the master bedroom. He threw out one, and Tudi said, "We want this one."

And he said, "Really! I almost didn't bring that one because Shelly has it."

Tudi repeated, "We like that one."

So they picked up all the carpet samples and went into the other rooms to make the other selections. Tudi selected them in an hour for the whole house.

The designer said, "All right, let me find out their availability."

The fact that he hadn't checked if those carpets were actually available should have set off alarm bells, but it didn't. What did we know, anyway? We were new at the game of rug roulette. Still, he called a few days later with the good news that everything was available. The first half of the order would be there in three weeks and the other half in four weeks. Okay, great.

About two and a half weeks later his assistant called: "There's a mix-up." I asked what he meant. The assistant said the carpet people hadn't ordered the carpets, and when questioned about why not, the carpet people said, "What do you mean? We never heard from you. So we never ordered those."

Tom came back with, "I have a faxed copy of the check that Tudi and Richard's accountant sent to you."

"Well, I haven't got a check," said the carpet people.

Historic Building Blunders
Congressional Office Buildings

We weren't the only people who had carpeting troubles. The U.S. Congress had trouble with carpets and other things too. The so-called New Senate Office Building, or the Dirksen Building, which provides offices for some senators and their staff, also provides many jokes about construction blunders. It is the most expensive office building ever built in the history of mankind, replacing the previous winner, the Rayburn Congressional Office Building, on the other side of Capitol Hill. The Dirksen Building cost just under three times the original bid, which is exactly what the Karn home

We went to the accountant, and he said, "I never got the okay to send it."

As was often the case in our odyssey of remodeling, it was everybody's fault and nobody's fault. Curly, Larry, and Moe would be proud.

"How long will it take to get the carpets?" Tudi asked Tom. "Eight weeks."

Apparently, these carpets had suddenly become very popular, because two and a half weeks before it was only going to be three or four weeks to deliver them. Now, unexpectedly, the remodeling cost—just under three times the original bid!

The contractor on the Rayburn Building made so much profit for the general contractor that he was able to buy the Philadelphia Eagles professional football team. In the Rayburn Building there were goofs galore, including building little kitchenettes for each office suite without plumbing for water. In the Dirksen Building, the main clock mounted on the building had metal hands that were so elaborate and heavy that the clock mechanism could not move them. Almost prophetically, in the building that housed stodgy old senators, time stood still. Then there were the very expensive linoleum floors that were very slippery and had senators and staff, again prophetically, falling down everywhere. They solved this problem by laying very expensive carpeting on top of the linoleum. Unfortunately, the carpeting was not only posh and expensive, it was thick and made it impossible to open the doors. So the doors had to be removed and redone.

wait had escalated to eight weeks. Tudi wasn't pleased. She said, "That is unacceptable. Bring me samples. We'll start over."

Tom brought carpet samples similar to the ones Tudi picked before, and I said, "Whatever's available, get it."

It was like being in a bar at closing time—you're no longer that particular.

The designer, calling from our house said "A" was available. We could have it in two weeks. "Okay, take that."

So that was done, except a couple days later he called and said, "They lied to me, it's not available."

"Well, what about 'B'?"

"I have to find out about 'B.'"

This had gotten so aggravating that we were on the verge of calling carpet people up even if we could only argue with their voice-mail answering machines.

This is when I said, "Honey, I'll fix it. We're going to look for ourselves. You can't tell me we can't get carpet in a few days. There are carpets all over this town. I know we're getting nice carpets, but you can't tell me that it's going to take eight weeks and it has to come from Italy. Ridiculous."

I felt proud of myself at that moment.

I asked Jeannie, the set decorator on *Home Improvement*, where to go for good carpet at a good price. I figured we couldn't go wrong asking a Jeannie. We got a sitter, went looking, and came back with two books of samples. We picked one.

Tudi called the designer and said we're going to do this.

He said, "Hold on, hold on. Let me bring you some samples on Monday. Some that I know are available."

What a concept! Now he *knows* of carpeting that's available! We ended up with carpeting similar to what we found ourselves, but it still took a week. What should have been a simple decision became a fiasco and weeks of trauma.

The
Chronology
of Change
Orders

Dad, please don't read this section!

Just as we parlayed across the country from New York to Los Angeles in a variation of the famous baseball double play, Tinkers to Evers to Chance, our remodeling odyssey became another multiple play from window to plaster to roof to everything else.

We didn't contemplate doing a complete tear-down and starting from ground zero. Here is the original bid on remodeling the house based on our first plan and the original specifications we decided upon:

Carpet Allowance $9,600
Ceramic Tile $9,263
Concrete $9,850
Demolition. $9,885
Drywall. $3,875
Electrical $11,750
Finish Carpentry. $18,834
Finish Hardware. $2,342
Fireplace $2,325
General conditions. $13,972
Glass & Glazing. $14,422
Gutters/Downspouts/Sheet Metal. $3,810
Hardwood Flooring $11,880
HVAC (Heating and Air Conditioning). $8,785
Insulation $785
Millwork. $5,800
Miscellaneous Steel $2,865
Painting $18,600

Plaster $4,320
Plumbing $5,522
Roofing. $31,985
Rough Carpentry. $38,809
Shower Enclosure/Accessories $2,207
Wood Doors & Frames. $12,396
Subtotal $253,882
Overhead $25,388
Profit $17,771
TOTAL **$297,041**

And here's a list of all the Change Orders to our original plan, starting with Change Order #1, the new windows:

1. Remove and replace existing windows with true-divided lights.
2. Furnish and install French doors, sidelights, and transoms, complete.
3. Remove and replace existing slab at pool room.
4. Relocate waste vent and water lines at pool room. Furnish and install new one-inch copper line to irrigation values.
5. Relocate existing electrical wiring at pool room.
6. Furnish and install 1½-inch gas line from new meter location to house.
7. Furnish and install new rafter tails and restucco entire house.
8. Remove existing roof structure and properly reframe.
9. Furnish and install casement windows in lieu of double hung.
10. Furnish and install four (4) new windows in living room.
11. Furnish and install stain grade fir windows in lieu of paint grade in family room, media office, and master bedroom.
12. Furnish and install mahogany French doors and sidelights in lieu of paint grade.

13. Furnish and install one (1) 6' x 6'8" x 1¾" 10 light mahogany French doors, and one (1) 2'8" x 6'8" x 1¾" 10 light mahogany French doors including mahogany casing and hardware.
14. Additional structural upgrades for 1,000 lbs./sq. roofing.
15. Not accepted. (AH-HA, SAVED MONEY!)
16. Furnish and install new beams, and paint grade tongue and groove ceiling in family room.
17. Reframe dining room ceiling.
18. Reframe kitchen ceiling.
19. Raise ceiling in maid's room and add beams.
20. Furnish and install two-zone HVAC system in maid's room.
21. Repipe north wing of home, complete.
22. Remove deficient gas line, furnish and install new gas line.
23. Repipe main house in type-L copper.
24. Furnish and install Redlands roof tile in lieu of Claylite.
25. Remodel vestibule/powder bath at media/office.
26. Remodel guest bath at front bedroom.
27. Not accepted.
28. Build custom cupola at garage roof.
29. Remodel master bathroom complete.
30. Remodel closets at upstairs guest bedroom. Furnish and install two (2) doors and one (1) window.
31. Additional electrical lighting and circuitry.
32. Additional doors/frames/hardware.
33. Copper gutters and downspouts.
34. Millwork at pool table room (less $5,800 allowance).
35. Reimbursement of building permit fee.
36. Plaster/tile fireplace in family room.
37. Entertainment center in family room.
38. Replace fan/coil unit for master bedroom zone and add humidifier.
39. Add skylight at master patio, change sizes, add custom white glass.

40. Remodel powder bath.
41. Remodel laundry room.
42. Various plumbing changes.
43. Interior plastering complete.
44. 75-gallon water heater.
45. Casing/baseboard.
46. Kitchen south wall remodel.
47. Add three plaster niches.
48. Changes to custom cabinetry @ pool table room.
49. Stain-grade beams and ceilings.
50. Upgrade master bath Pullman allowance.
51. Lath/plaster chimney surrounds.
52. Q-Lon weather-stripping.
53. Delete ceramic tile material.
54. Custom tile installation.
55. Tumbled marble @ kitchen/laundry/rear entry.
56. Redo two (2) showers.
57. Furnish and install copper leaderheads.
58. Remove and replace subfloor at kitchen/laundry.
59. Additional roof tile.
60. Build plaster arch @ master bedroom.
61. 1½ inch bull-nose and plaster @ two (2) fireplaces.
62. Replaster chimney caps.
63. Additional general conditions.
64. Site wall and fencing modifications.
65. Furnish and install masonry @ five (5) patio/stoops.
66. Add plaster detail @ equipment well wall.
67. Fabricate and install island cabinet.
68. Fabricate and install cabinet over armoire.
69. Furnish and install additional shelf, pole, and shoe racks.
70. Furnish and install paint grade crown molding (not accepted).
71. Install owner-supplied plumbing fixtures @ upstairs baths (not accepted).

72. Additional preparation/priming/painting (less material credit).
73. Fabricate and install two (2) cabinets @ master suite.
74. Delete hardwood floors.
75. Fabricate and reinstall copper elbows @ all downspouts.
76. Furnish and install tapered poly-columns in lieu of wood.
77. Delete carpet allowance.
78. Fabricate and install Alder stain-grade cabinetry throughout master closet.
79. Fabricate and install custom red oak stair and railing, including ceramic tile risers.
80. Changes to custom cabinetry @ pool table room.
81. Additional tile and limestone installations.
82. Additional electrical items.
83. Modifications to existing kitchen cabinetry.
84. Rebuild wine rack cabinet.
85. Delete finish hardware.
86. Additional finish carpentry items.
87. Prep, prime, and paint laundry, hallway, and bath cabinets, and additional painting and finishing.
88. Furnish and install select rough-sawn cedar @ media office ceiling (replace damaged ceiling).
89. Delete shower enclosures from base bid.

You can see why I had to brush up on my speed reading so I could get through all the details of the Change Order paperwork.

As you can calculate, the windows decision led to about $150,000 in additional expense on the remodeling for the windows and the resulting stucco, roof, and other changes. Looking at the list now, I'm reminded that, before the remodeling, we would often kiss our money good-bye for some purchase we made, but during the remodeling we didn't even get a chance to whisper in its ear.

Historic Building Blunders
The Second-Richest Man

Just so you don't think I am the Change Order king of the world, consider the case of Hassanal Bolkiah, the fifty-two-year-old Sultan of Brunei and, until recently, the richest man in the world, with a fortune estimated at $36 billion. Difficult as it is to believe that a man worth $36 billion could have problems, the sultan is going through hard times. For one thing, the sharp drop in oil prices and the shaking economy in Asia has him slipping toward the poor house and downgraded to the second richest man in the world, with Bill Gates, from my hometown of Seattle, moving into the numero uno spot with a net worth of $70 billion. Besides that, the sultan has trouble with his free-spending, X-rated brother, Prince Jefri, and Jefri's son, Prince Hakeem, who is involved in some massive remodeling projects of his own. The most notable is the Jerudong Hotel in Brunei (a country on the northern shore of the island of Borneo).

The Jerudong Hotel is already a huge white elephant that has cost $700 million and may never be finished. Prince Hakeem likes to zip around the construction site in his Range Rover issuing change orders left, right, and in between. For example, when he found that his Range Rover SUV was too wide

in the World

for the golf-cart paths, he ordered the paths widened. That meant the entire water filtration system for the golf course had to be reengineered, dug up, and reconstructed. When Hakeem discovered that his beloved Range Rover could barely squeeze between the hotel and the adjacent auditorium building, he ordered the entire auditorium moved over five feet so it wouldn't scratch his SUV. For the hotel lobby, he ordered a four-story-high plate-glass window created. This had to be specially made and imported, and it is the only one of its kind in the world because it is also very thick. The extreme thickness is necessary because human managers will keep the air-conditioned temperature on one side of the glass at 62 degrees inside the hotel lobby, while God lets the temperature soar to a very humid 100+ degrees on the other side of the glass.

Looking Back a Year Later

The Mystical, Magical Mistake Tour

A year later Tudi and I can start from the kitchen and wander through the downstairs of the house toward the master bedroom, citing all the glitches, goofs, and goblins we encountered. Yes, while it may be hard to believe, it did not all turn out perfectly.

Kitchen goofs that we didn't realize until we lived with them for a while begin with the dishwasher, which was both what Tudi wanted and what she didn't want. In our previous house, we had a dishwasher that squeaked and mumbled and rolled as it went along, and we thought, "Great, we can start fresh with a soundproof, high-tech dishwasher." We went to the appliance store, got a top-of-the-line dishwasher, and had it installed.

Tudi was clear on what she wanted: "I wanted something very quiet, and it is. However, I didn't take my dishes with me to see how they would fit in there. Because it's insulated for sound, the dish space is inadequate and inconvenient. For example, there are only six proper spaces for plates in this dishwasher, and if you have, say, eight people over, you have to do some maneuvering to make everything fit. I know now I'd rather have more noise and better space.

"It also seems that the plumbing in the laundry room is somehow connected to the vegetable sink in the kitchen. When the clothes washer is running, it gurgles a lot in the vegetable sink and makes it stinky in the kitchen. We asked the plumber to look at it, and he said, 'Well, there isn't a whole lot we can do about it.'"

Then there was the cabinet problem. When we added the tongue-and-groove to the back, it took up depth in the shelves. Only later did Tudi discover she couldn't buy a set of new dishes she liked because the new dinner plates were twelve inches in diameter and the cabinets would only hold eleven-inch dishes.

Moving from the kitchen to Cooper's playroom, there's the case of the plantation shutters. These were something from the old house that we liked and wanted to keep, even though, in the back of our minds, we knew that they weren't quite right. We still justified holding on to them because we liked them and thought we could make them work, but as the house progressed, in the Spanish Mediterranean style, it was clear that the plantation shutters did not go with that. So they're still sitting in the garage.

A lot of times in remodeling you'll encounter details that you really like and feel you should keep. But if the house style changes drastically and, even though you still like that detail, it's not going to fit, you still can't justify throwing it away. So it sits in the garage, and then four years later you go, "Well, you know what? Let's dump that stuff," and you get rid of it even though it's something you kept for four years and you really like it. There comes a point when you have to throw it out, and throwing it out makes you feel good. You should keep these things for future good feelings.

If it wasn't for the last minute, nothing would get done.

Another glitch we have a year later relates to the sliding pocket doors in Cooper's bathroom and in the laundry room. Because of the limited space in that bathroom, we decided to use sliding pocket doors that slip into the wall, instead of hinged doors. Pocket doors are great, but if you don't do them right, they'll scrape or not go in the correct depth. This one doesn't hang just right. It wobbles. Similar thing in the laundry room, where the door goes back in the wall too deep and you have trouble fishing it out. Pocket doors are a tricky thing.

Then we had the glitch in Cooper's toy closet. I came in one day to instruct the working crew about what I wanted in closet design and said I want a shelf here, a shelf there, and so on. We did about eight closets in about thirty minutes because by then I was like, "This is what I want. Do it." Cooper has two closets in his room and one of them is just for toys. I don't know if we ever discussed it, or nobody thought about it, but there's no light in the toy closet. That's another OOPS! oversight."

In the master bedroom we had them build a fireplace so we could enjoy cozy nights even when it's raining outside (only rarely in California). Besides the aesthetics of looking good and providing supplemental heat, we found we had the added advantage of being able to hear the pitter-pat amplified through our brand-new chimney. That's because of the metal chimney cap and spark arrester. At first it was a little disconcerting, and we asked what we could do about it and were told they would "look into it." Now, a year later, it has become part of the sounds of our new home, and we need it to fall asleep and miss it when it's not raining. It's like the story of the Arkansas traveler who spent a rainy night with a man in his leaky cabin. The man explained that he couldn't go up on the roof to fix it when it was raining, and when it wasn't raining, the roof didn't need fixing.

Another thing we were reminded of in the master bathroom is that houses breathe. They expand in the summertime and contract in the wintertime. You can usually tell by doors that are harder to close, and that's what happened with the door to the infamous shower that had the huge bench. Apparently, the metal expanded and now the shower door is hard to close. Maybe we should have left that big bench in there so we could rest after trying to close the door. Oh, well . . .

And remember that pronounced carpet seam in the master bedroom? We talked about covering a lot of it with an area rug in front of the fireplace, and we still intend to do it, but a year later we still haven't.

So, here again is that important remodeling lesson: you will change your mind about looks, textures, finishes, arrangements, and a lot of other stuff as you go along. Nothing is set in concrete. Tudi had trouble in the dining room with colors, and with light switches in the pool table room that we still haven't corrected a year later. Still another remodeling lesson: whatever you put off until "later" happens *much* later or, even, never.

We lucked out pretty well on most of the appliances we installed, with the notable exception being a humidifier. The salesman assured me it would work religiously, and he was right. It never turns on unless the house is as hot as hell or it's a Sunday.

There is one thing about the room upstairs that's now my office and workroom. I regret that I didn't get the workmen to redo the shelving in the closet. Now, a year later, it's just the same as it was at the beginning, and it's not practical. You know, we got tired of it all. Tired of decisions. Tired of change. Tired of all of it.

Fatigue is a major factor. At some point you just decide you're tired of the whole routine and you want it done. When that fatigue walks in the door, the rest of your good intentions fly out the window (along with the firemen!).

Now What?

I know in the back of my mind I want to do the outdoors—landscaping, so we can use the motto of the U.S., namely, in sod we trust—and I want to redo the pool.

The fact is, when you're remodeling and restuccoing and all of that, the outside foliage gets pummeled, trampled on, and murdered. It gets tied back, and eventually much of it comes back, but I still want to do a lot more with dramatic lighting and different kinds of trees and bushes that flower during various seasons so you always have something blooming in the yard. So you don't have everything blooming all at once, and then, a few weeks later, you have nothing.

The outside of the house looks wonderful. The red tile roof made a big difference; the copper gutters made a difference; and so do the decorative pillars around the house. The first idea that Tom and I came up with was that they should be fluted. Every pillar I'd seen in my entire life was fluted, so I didn't know there would be that many straight pillars out there.

We talked about it and he said fluted pillars would be $1,200, and I figured that wasn't too bad for the dozen or so I wanted until he clarified that it was $1,200 *each*, or about $14,000 for the dozen pillars. That's an awful lot for just fluting. I mean, for that price I would have expected the entire symphony orchestra. So we explored alternatives.

Tom said, "I can get you straight pillars for three hundred dollars apiece."

"Wait a minute. There's a nine hundred dollar difference between fluted and straight?"

"Yup."

"Why?"

(Silence)

"Go with the straight. I'm not going to pay twelve hundred dollars for fluting."

An interesting thing about fluting pillars is that it goes back to the Greeks, who were famous for the fluted pillars all around their temples and buildings. There's an optical illusion in that, if you have a straight, plain pillar, it seems wrong to your eyes. That's why they have them fluted. There's some-

Historic Building Blunders
The Kudzu Mistake

Man's development mistakes are not always in bricks and mortar. For example, in the southern states fifty years ago, farmers and landscape architects were worked up about erosion-depleted and washed-out soil. Then came the "miracle of kudzu," an Asian crawling vine that has broad leaves and a thick stem that gripped the loose soil and stopped erosion on farms, as well as decorative banks around homes and commercial building and other slopes. It also enriched the barren soil with nitrogen, a natural fertilizer.

Today, the miracle has become a scourge because kudzu is all they said it was and too much more. It does grow, but it

thing in the curvature of your eye that makes it align more and makes the fluted pillar look right. It is visually more pleasing to the eye.

We went to Disneyland, and everywhere in Disneyland are these overfluted pillars. We thought, "Oh, let's do the fluted. We'll pay the extra money." Then Tom found this company that did fluted columns in a plastic compound for $300. So we got what we wanted. Of course, we had to go through the anxiety. Always have to go through anxiety. They were ordered, installed, and our wonderful artist from Kentucky, Esther, was able to create the finishing touches. She's great.

As originally designed, the garage doors had a big X hatch

grows too wide and far and fast. It does stop erosion, but it also is so thick it chokes out other vegetation, including decorative flower beds, hedges, and ornamental plants. Here are the amazing statistics: one kudzu plant will start growing in the summer and will cover sixty feet in every direction four feet deep! Every spring it starts growing all over again, adding to its growth the season before. It sweeps over and, literally, engulfs everything in its path: fences, poles, furniture, cars, buildings, gardens—everything. It's like something out of an old Japanese horror movie because nothing seems to stop it— chain saws, axes, fire, and most chemicals. Finally, in recent years Dow Chemical came up with Tordon 10K, which will kill kudzu roots if you consciously apply the chemical in both spring and fall. Even so, it may never be eradicated since it already covers millions of acres of ground—some of it inaccessible.

design on them, making them look more equestrian than Spanish Mediterranean. However, they were topped by a nice-looking arch pattern. We hated the X and loved the arch and, with the help of the Wayne-Dalton garage-door people, we filled in and eliminated the X's while keeping the arch pattern. It really looks much better, plus the automatic Wayne-Dalton garage-door openers possess an unusual security feature not found on most such remote devices. The Wayne-Dalton opener automatically changes its code number every time you use it, making it almost impossible for a stranger to get your code and break into the garage.

In the remodeling, we always tried to incorporate some of our son's ideas, but we may have to draw the line on some of his visions, such as the one about a moat surrounding the house with a seventy-five-foot swimming pool slide that spits you out of a clown's mouth. However, there is a child in all of us, and the idea of putting in a natural rock waterfall with a natural rock slide would be more appropriate.

We also want a spa that's more user friendly. A lot of times

Historic Building Blunder
I.U. Library

The Main Library at Indiana University sinks over an inch every year because, when it was built, engineers failed to take into account the weight of all the books that would occupy the building.

when you buy a house, you also inherit things that are a little hard to figure out how to work. The spa we got with this house is foreign to me. I've had trouble getting the heater and the jets to work the way I want them to. I suppose we could have six friends come over and sit on the edge of the pool kicking feverishly, or fill the spa with Perrier water with all the bubbles so we could swim in the water and drink it too.

On the house, I can't think of what else we would want to do. It's all pretty much here. We have to furnish the living room and find a workable layout. The fact that we don't have living room furniture a year and a half later is a tribute to the exhaustion from making architectural detail decision making. Now we don't want to decide what kind of furniture to put in the living room. That's harder for me to do—to visualize that. Some people are just good at it; I'm not. My mom was great for that kind of stuff. Our walls at home were never bare because she had paintings up, and she also had furniture arranged. I acquired some of that, but now, because I labored over getting walls of a certain texture and color, I'm reluctant to hang a picture where I might not want it later. If I did that, I would have to repair the stucco. However, a fresh tube of Crest toothpaste can solve that—just make sure you don't get the blue gel kind. And fluoride is optional.

We began our gigantic remodeling project on September 5, 1996, and I expected we would probably be done by Christmas. In reality, I don't think we even had our building permits by Christmas and we finished most of the project (there's always something else) in October of 1997.

Our son viewed the whole experience through the eyes of a perceptive innocent. He said, "Dad, I don't get it."

"What?"

"Why do you buy a house and then tear it down and then build it again?"

His mother said, "Good question."

I told him, "You know how sometimes you'll build something with your Legos and then you want to add something to it or change the design? You have to tear it down and build it up again."

Thank goodness he didn't ask why we hadn't built the house out of Lego blocks.

He accepted that. Now that it's over, so do we. The real test that will make you feel good about remodeling is to go out home shopping and see what a comparable house would cost you.

In the end, we know there are five steps to remodeling: Dreams, Hope, Frustration, Poverty, and Thank God it's done.

Appendixes

Appendix A

Rick's Home Remodeler's Survival Guide

Rick's Rules

1. How to pick a remodeling contractor according to the experts is similar to the way we actually did it. The professionals say the best way to find a remodeling contractor is through referrals by people you know.

2. Rick's hover rule: try to be on the remodeling site as often and for as long as you can. Contractors and subcontractors don't think the way your wife does. They want to get "it" done. She wants "it" to work and be out of sight. That's why there's no light switch in the laundry room and you can't open the bathroom window. You need to be there to clarify exactly what it is you want done, assuming that you know what you want done.

3. The most important part of remodeling is done before a toolbox is opened. It is carefully drawn and starts with very detailed plans, specs, and a contract. As with many people who remodel, we started that way, but kept making changes as we thought of great new ideas.

4. Keep a diary, audio tape, and photo album or videotape.

5. Check the work constantly and carefully. Don't be afraid to stop the work if it is not being done the way you want it. You are going to live with it, the work crew is not.

6. Occasionally take a breather away from the house to keep your perspective. This seems like a contradiction to Rule #2, which is all the more reason for having it; it's vital to ensure your sanity.

7. Challenge bids. I did and got a lower price almost every time.

8. You should head for the door when the contractor:
  a. Has an address or phone number you cannot verify
  b. Has only two main assets: a pickup and a cell phone
  c. Can't give you references of people he has worked for before
  d. Asks you to pay a big chunk of money up front
  e. Asks you to make the check payable to him personally or wants cash
  f. Gives you the "This price is only good for today" routine

9. Building-contractor warning lights. Be very careful with any contractor who:
  • Gives vague or reluctant answers to your questions
  • You can't get in touch with readily
  • Acts impatient and treats you as if you are stupid

10. A reality you must understand: there is a vast difference between what contractors will do and say to GET the job and what they will do and say when they are DOING the job.

11. Another reality: it is not unusual for contractors or subcontractors not to show up on the day and time they promised. The building business is semichaotic in nature and exact timetables are rare. To expect order and precision in building is not reasonable.

12. Get color samples for all painting, staining, etc., and keep them so you can compare them with the finished job.

13. You must keep your sense of humor. This isn't the White

House or the Pharaoh's pyramids and mistakes will be made. You must learn to laugh or you're doomed to cry. Tudi would sometimes cry and I would pace. I am a pacer, not a yeller. Always, we would get through the problem and end up accepting the inevitable and laughing. It's the only way to make it through.

14. It is helpful if you have a basic understanding of blueprints. It's a foreign language, just like learning to read music, but you need to try if you're going to enjoy the melody. More important! If you're not absolutely clear about what any of the lines, symbols, notations, and other stuff on the blueprint mean— ASK. We are all stupid, just about different things, and there's no shame in asking to have something on the blueprint explained to you.

As Tudi says, "I wish I would have communicated more and earlier. Then we wouldn't have had to go back and redo so much. I wish I had understood the documents better. Sometimes the designer would explain things and I would think I understood, but I really didn't. I didn't know that I didn't understand and he didn't know it either."

15. Always remember: it's your house and it's your money. No question is stupid if you don't know the answer.

16. Understand the Domino Theory. Nothing you do in a remodeling happens in a vacuum. If you do A, it will change B and C, so find out about what changes B and C will be, will cost, and whether that's what you want. Everything you do interconnects with something else in the house. There's a lot of omission when talking about one aspect of the job. I don't think it's necessarily intentional, it's just that the builder is focusing on what you're asking or talking about and not bringing up all the other effects that will come of it. This might also be called "Dem Bones" in action. You remember, "The foot bone is connected to the ankle bone and the ankle bone is connected to the leg bone and the leg bone is connected to the thigh bone . . . " Too often, however, none of these is connected to the brain bone.

17. Your ideas are just as important and valid as those of the designer or contractor. A lot of great ideas come from the lay person. You may say, "I see this or I want to do that," and sometimes the designer or architect might cringe, but that doesn't mean your idea isn't valid. So if you believe in it, stick with it. That's how new styles are created. It's like blackened food. You know, someone didn't invent blackened chicken. They burned it because it wasn't a good piece of chicken or fish. It was a cheaper piece of fish that they burned so you wouldn't see the imperfections. And now blackened fish is a delicacy.

18. Remodeling vs. Tearing Down is a key question. Sometimes it makes more sense to level the house and start from scratch, just as Tom said earlier about the alternatives when we first began exploring the remodeling:

"The concept of paying the enormous prices one pays in this city for a house only to tear it down is not something people quickly decide on doing. Still, with all the problems we often run into with remodeling an existing house, leveling the old house and starting new is the way to go sometimes. It might go faster and cost less—maybe.

"With Rick and Tudi's house, we didn't start with that point of view. Admittedly, it's a very difficult point of view for anyone to swallow when they've just purchased the house to say, 'Let's knock it down.' Very few people could grasp that easily."

The answer, of course, depends on the individual and why he's buying the house. Is it, for example, to live in forever, or to spruce up and resell? Everything is relevant and relative to each individual. If you're buying something to fix it up to sell, then you have to think about what will add to the resale value. There are wonderful books out there explaining what would be a good thing to do for resale . . . maybe not touch the upstairs, but put in a new island in the kitchen.

On the other hand, if you're going to live there yourself, there will be certain things you want that are unique to you and your lifestyle. The owner before us was a marriage counselor, and had a soundproof room built at some expense so his clients could rant and holler without disturbing the rest of the household or the neighbors. Of course, that might be good for some married couples anyhow.

So everything is relevant and it depends on how much money you have to spend. You know, I was fortunate in that I could spend, not an exorbitant amount of money, but the money to do something I really wanted to do and use nice materials. There's also something wonderful in spending less on materials that look just as good. There's a certain pride in being able to do something a little less expensively where the outcome will be the same.

Appendix B

Rick's List of Mistakes You'll Make

From years of experience, remodelers and home improvement stores know that the homeowner will usually make one of several common mistakes when buying or ordering material for his home. Here they are for you to learn before you live them:

Always Measure and Re-Measure

The worse thing is to order something to fit a place in your house and find out it's too big or too small when you get it home. The cheapest frustration insurance is a tape measure. They're worth many times what you will pay for them, and some building suppliers give out yardsticks for free! BUT there is one important secret about this secret: don't measure once—measure twice to double check. Even better, have someone else measure and confirm your figures. If it's an expensive project or it's going to actually be built by a professional, pay a little extra for the pro to do the measuring. That way he's responsible for mistakes, not you.

A Picture Is Worth It

A simple but little followed secret is to give the person filling your order a picture or sketch of what you have in mind. Also, bring in a sample of what you want. This is particularly helpful with colors because the light is different everywhere and it affects how the colors appear.

The Secret of Batch Numbers

Many products are identified by numbers, such as paints and tiles. So whenever you have painting done by a pro, ask him for the brand name and the batch number of the paint he's using, in case you have to duplicate it later. Same with tiles. Get the manufacturer's name and batch number. If the store you go to can't duplicate it, call around to find a store or the manufacturer, who can.

Left and Right Handed

As we were reminded with the shower door in our son's playroom, all the doors on cabinets, showers, etc. are either "right hand" or "left hand." If you face the door, the side on which the opening handle or knob is tells you which it is. If the handle or knob is on the right as you face the door, it's a "right hand" door, and the reverse if the handle or knob is on the left as you face it.

The Sink, Tub, and Toilet Mysteries

There are a wide variety of sinks, tubs, and toilets, and that means you must be careful in checking what you need for your home. Check the number of holes in each and what side they're on to see that it's correct for the pipes, outlets, and drains at your house. Measure the length, width, and depth of sinks and tubs to make sure they'll fit. Also, check how far from the back wall the unit should be. This is particularly true of toilets.

Toilets are odd because they come in different heights, and you may not realize that until you get it home. Also, toilet seats are usually sold separately and cannot be returned, so be sure you get what you want before you leave the store.

Finally, Check the Store's Return or Refund Policy

If you get it home and it isn't right, you don't want the surprise of having to pay full price for the correct replacement.

Appendix C

Rick's Humorous Home Buyer's Vocabulary

A humorous play on words common to home ownership, remodeling, and other bizarre human endeavors:

ABSTRACT (OF TITLE)
A vague concept about who owns what, that is as clear to the average person as the other abstracts, such as in a Picasso painting.

ACCELERATION CLAUSE
This means the bank can require you to pay off the mortgage immediately under certain conditions, such as the scales in Pisces being out of balance or the White Sox being in the World Series.

AMORTIZATION
This comes from the Latin *amorte* (to die) and describes your condition when you figure out how much you will pay in total on your mortgage. It's like two or three times the original balance.

APPRAISAL
From the Latin *appraizarion*, meaning to tell you it's a lovely home and you made a good choice. Commonly used by friends and relatives who don't want to hurt your feelings or tell you about the toxic waste dump down the block.

ASSUMPTION OF MORTGAGE

This is your belief or assumption that the bank loaning you the money is going to be fair to you.

BROKER

This is the person who convinces you to buy this place immediately no matter what you have to pay. She or he is the broker and you are the brokee.

BUILDING LINE

The line of hype and salesmanship that convinces you to expand your original plan from a minor touch-up to a major construction project in the class of the Three Gorges dam or the Denver airport. Comparable to the kind of line used with success near closing time in local bars where indefinable pleasures are promised for relative small investment.

CERTIFICATE OF TITLE

This is an expensive opinion from a lawyer that essentially says he doesn't know of any reason why the present owner of the house can't sell it to you. Admittedly, there may be plenty of reasons why he can't sell you the house, but the lawyer is just saying he doesn't know of them. In brief, this is a piece of paper you pay a lawyer that tells you the lawyer is stupid, uninformed, or doesn't care.

CLOSING COSTS

If you thought the price of the house was high, wait until you see the list of "closing costs." These are all the fees, taxes, and do-wa-diddies that the bank, broker, escrow officer, and their relatives can dream up. This list makes the Pentagon procurement office look frugal. It is why escrow offices secretly keep defibrillation machines handy in order to resuscitate stunned buyers.

CLOSING DAY

A day set aside by the seller, broker, and escrow people to break out the bubbly and celebrate finally selling this house.

CLOUD

A frown that passes over your face as you read the escrow documents, which appear to be written in English but which you are embarrassed to admit are incomprehensible to you or your spouse. The choice at this point is to look stupid or be cool and cheated.

COMMISSION

As in the phrase "commission of a robbery," this is the amount of money to be divided up among the listing broker, the selling broker, the selling broker's ex-wife and bookie, the child support people, the car dealer, and other assorted creditors who the broker has been stalling while he or she convinced you what a great buy you were getting.

CONDEMNATION

A common form of speech resorted to by many new property owners upon discovering the termite infestation, flooded basement, cracked foundation, sagging timbers, and assorted other shortcomings that neither the broker nor the property inspector seemed to mention.

CONDOMINIUM

Formerly mistaken for something men carried in their wallets but now referring to a type of apartment multiple ownership where everything is either your private property or part of the "common area" and the responsibility of the condominium organization. Almost always, everything that goes wrong and needs repair is limited to your private area by the twisted definitions in the condominium documents that you either didn't read or did read but didn't understand.

CONVENTIONAL MORTGAGE

This is a loan for part of the market value of the house. If you are eligible for a mortgage guaranteed by the government, your property doesn't have to be worth more than the mortgage. This doesn't make good business sense, but it makes good politics for people who want your vote.

DEED

This is a piece of paper that says you own a piece of dirt. It is probably the most expensive piece of paper you will ever own.

DEED OF TRUST

This is a misnomer since the word "trust" should never be uttered in connection with a real estate transaction.

DEFAULT

This is a word used to introduce blame to an incompetent real estate person, contractor, or previous owner, as in "Default is Mr. Anderson's."

DOCUMENTARY STAMPS

The state charges a tax when real estate is sold, and this is paid by buying documentary stamps and sticking them on the deed. No one has dared to mention in the last two hundred years that, when the British Parliament passed a similar Stamp Act, it triggered the American Revolutionary War.

DOWN PAYMENT

The amount of money between what the bank will put up and the price of the house. Roughly equivalent to all the money you have in your savings account, if you're lucky.

EARNEST MONEY

The deposit money given to the seller to make him feel better, and that makes you feel nervous. So far as we can determine, no one who has ever paid this has been named Ernest.

ENCROACHMENT

They will tell you this means something that intrudes on your property such as roaches and termites.

ENCUMBRANCE

This is something that reduces your claim on the property and gives you the shivers, which is why the term is derived from "cucumber," as in "ice cold as a cucumber."

EQUITY

This is the actors' union, to which you can qualify for membership if you can pretend that you're calm throughout your escrow performance and understand every document you signed.

ESCROW

A mysterious and obscure process by which money and deeds change hands. It can be either a noun or a verb, depending on what's happening to you.

FORECLOSURE
A process by which your property is taken away from you. Contrary to rumor, there is no connection with the term *foreskin*.

GRANTEE
This is you, the buyer. Grantee is a distortion of the original term, "Groanee."

GRANTOR
This is the seller, and it comes from the famous Civil War general and president, Ulysses S. Grant, who was noted for consuming vast quantities of alcohol, which is what the seller does in celebration after unloading the property on you.

LIEN
This is the sagging state of buyers upon emerging from escrow, when they must often hold onto a wall to steady themselves.

MORTGAGE COMMITMENT
The word "commitment" is associated with confinement into a mental institution, which seems indicated for anyone who reads and understands the loan papers and signs them anyhow.

PLAT
A map of the property you're buying. Also, your financial condition after buying and remodeling it: plat broke.

POINTS
This has many fancy and fanciful definitions, but it is essentially a bribe paid to the bank so it will loan you money at outrageous terms which you will spend the next many years struggling to repay.

REAL ESTATE BROKER
A middle man or agent who sells real estate on a commission basis. The broker does not have title to the property, but generally represents the owner. His or her main job is to bamboozle you into thinking he or she is looking out for *your* best interests.

RESTRICTIVE COVENANTS
A list of activities forbidden to you on the property you just bought. This might include voodoo rituals, singing the aria from *La Boheme* at midnight, repairing your car on the front lawn, and killing chickens on Sunday. These, of course, are permitted to most normal, free Americans, but not you.

TAX
Payment you must make to the state for the privilege of paying to the bank and adhering to all the restrictive covenants.

TITLE
Either the right of ownership or the name applied to you, such as "home owner" and "lord of the manor," which is sometimes mispronounced as lord of the manure.

TITLE INSURANCE
This is the only insurance in the world issued for events that have already happened, and it simply says, "We have checked and nobody has filed a paper affecting your ownership. If we're wrong, we pay you damages for our failure to check the records accurately."